UNSUNG HEROINES
THE WOMEN
WHO WON THE WAR

UNSUNG HEROINES

The Women Who Won the War

VERA LYNN

with Robin Cross and Jenny de Gex

ISIS
LARGE PRINT
Oxford, England
Santa Barbara, California

First published in Great Britain 1990
by Sidgwick & Jackson Ltd

Published in Large Print 1991 by Clio Press,
55 St. Thomas' Street, Oxford OX1 1JG,
by arrangement with Sidgwick & Jackson Ltd

British Library Cataloguing in Publication Data
Lynn, Vera
Unsung heroines : the women who won the war.
I. Title II. Cross, Robin, *1948-*
III. de Gex, Jenny
940.084

ISBN 1-85089-596-1

Printed and bound by Hartnolls Ltd, Bodmin, Cornwall
Cover designed by CGS Studios, Cheltenham

CONTENTS

Introduction by Vera Lynn

Authors' Note

1 The Road to War 1

2 Under Fire

    The Storm Breaks 25

    The Battle of Britain 49

    The Blitz 55

3 Into Uniform 72

4 Backs to the Land 102

5 The Secret War

    Intelligence 116

    Resistance 131

6 Prisoners of Japan 160

7 Front Line Nurses 189

8 Seeing it Through 216

    Acknowledgements 229

    Bibliography 230

    Index 233

INTRODUCTION

When war broke out, my immediate reaction was that
Adolf Hitler had brought an end to my singing career.
I could never have imagined that in the succeeding years
I would be able to reach out to so many people, at
home and abroad, through radio. That was my war
effort, and it opened up a whole new world for me.

In Britain the war had a profound effect on women,
not just as victims but as active participants in the war
effort. Like me, many of them found new possibilities
and a new confidence in their war role, whether it was
in the Land Army, the Auxiliary Territorial Service, as
an Air Raid Warden or one of the voluntary services
which plugged so many of the caring gaps during the
wartime years. As the many women in the pages of this
book reveal, their wartime service brought a sense of
comradeship and fulfilment that would have been
unattainable in the pre-war years. Of course war also
brought separation and suffering to millions, and in the
occupied countries of Europe and the Far East many
women were put to the test in conditions of great
hardship and danger. Theirs is a story of quiet courage
and humanity.

In this book, a long-cherished project, we have
pulled together many of these strands to provide a
picture of women's wartime experience, seen through
their own eyes and told in their own words. In the
course of our research it has been a great pleasure and
privilege to meet and talk with so many splendid
women, and on occasion to find a connection between

their experience and my own. RAF nurse Iris Ogilvie and her colleague Mollie Giles were the first women to land on the Normandy beaches after D-Day, and the gruelling conditions they endured reminded me instantly of the trials and tribulations of touring the front line in Burma with ENSA in the autumn of 1944. Washing the day's grime off under canvas with a bucket of cold water was an experience we all shared.

It was also an intensely moving experience to travel to Belgium and Holland to meet such Resistance workers as Marie Eugénie-Jadoul, Nel Lind and Joke Folmer, all of whom suffered imprisonment at the hands of the Nazis. Their courage in the face of death is an example to us all. One of the many heartwarming aspects of the many post-war visits I have made to the countries occupied by the Nazis was the importance people attached to the BBC, whose broadcasts were seen as the voice of freedom. They even knew all the words of the songs I sang on my radio programme "Sincerely Yours".

Wartime diaries play an important part in *Unsung Heroines*. Sometimes the passion expressed in them made me feel like a trespasser in someone else's life. But they convey the true feeling of the time and we must be grateful that these women have chosen to recall their experiences, sometimes in the heat of the moment, sometimes later in tranquility. Not least among their many qualities is their eye for quirky detail, for the minutiae of life seen from a woman's point of view.

My only regret is that space has limited our choice from the treasure house of material gathered in by my collaborators Robin Cross and Jenny de Gex. I am greatly indebted to them for shaping this mass of information into a readable story and to our editor Esther Jagger for providing the essential finishing touches. A special thanks to the many people who have so freely given us their time and the benefit of their expertise, and to the women themselves.

Vera Lynn
August 1990

AUTHORS' NOTE

In recent years the role of women in World War II has increasingly become the focus of both scholarly attention and works of popular history. The feminist movement provided the initial impetus, seeking to reveal the "hidden history" all too often glossed over by conventional accounts of the war, and this has been followed by a stream of more accessible memoirs and studies of women's contribution to the war effort in the forces, factories and fields. Different writers may reach different conclusions, but the importance of the subject cannot be denied.

More than any other combatant in World War II, with the possible exception of the Soviet Union, Britain bent every sinew to the waging of Total War. The entire nation was embraced by the war effort and a substantial civilian part of it was propelled into the front line by the Luftwaffe's bombing campaign against Britain's cities. In the winter of 1940 a woman Air Raid Warden in Holborn or Stepney was in greater physical danger every night than the majority of men serving in the forces.

In the armed services, too, women not only released men for combat duty but also had a direct impact on the fighting of the war. The female personnel of the Mixed Batteries in Anti-Aircraft Command, and the women who served on over a thousand balloon sites, were at the sharp end of Britain's air defences against the Luftwaffe. It was a member of the Women's Auxiliary Air Force, Section Officer Constance

Babington Smith, who was the first to spot evidence of the V-weapons on photo-reconnaissance pictures of the research establishment at Peenemünde. Long before the plans for the Normandy invasion were realized, female SOE agents were fighting a secret war in Occupied Europe. A week after the D-Day landings in June 1944 two RAF nurses, Iris Ogilvie and Mollie Giles, were working in conditions of considerable danger in the Normandy beach-head.

Just as these provide significant points of detail in a far greater picture, so this book has attempted to draw together a range of women's wartime stories in a mosaic of their experience in the years 1939-45. This is a vast subject, whose surface can only be scratched by a single volume, and our choice has necessarily been selective. Some subjects which we covered in detail in our previous book *We'll Meet Again*, notably the domestic front and life in war-time industry, we have left for a future volume. This has been balanced by extending our focus beyond the British Isles to include chapters on Intelligence and Resistance and the experience of women interned by the Japanese.

Rather than bombard the reader with a succession of vivid "snap shots" of the war, we have attempted to let the majority of women in *Unsung Heroines* tell their stories at some length. In the process the incidental detail they reveal not only provides a valuable insight into the flavour of the war as it was experienced at the time but also interplays effectively with the contemporary interviews we have included, in which war is remembered with the advantage of hindsight.

The war brought with it suffering, bereavement and

horrors of all kinds. But for many women it was, quite literally, the experience of a lifetime which gave them opportunities which no one could have envisaged in the 1930s and confidence to face the problems of the post-war world. Susan Woolfitt, who in 1943 volunteered to work on an Inland Waterways narrow boat carrying cargo between London and the Midlands, spoke for many women when she wrote that her time on the "cut" was "the most interesting, original and enviable year of my life; a year that I never could have spent if it hadn't been for the war; a year that I wouldn't have missed for anything in the world . . . we were conscious that the war was still on, and that in our own line of country we were doing what we could to help win it. For so many millions of people all over the world the war brought horror, torture and loss, that it seems almost wrong to have found anything good in what it brought to me, but it would be less than honest not to admit that it *did* bring me good".

Making the final selection was an agonizing process — we could have filled a volume twice or even three times the size. We are greatly indebted to all the women who helped us and without whose advice, good will and good humour our task would have been impossible.

Robin Cross and Jenny de Gex

CHAPTER
ONE

The Road to War

The prospect of war hung heavily over Europe in the late 1930s. Anyone over the age of thirty had vivid memories of World War I, and the walking wounded of those terrible years — amputees and the victims of gas and shell shock — survived as reminders of the human waste caused by warfare.

Throughout this period Adolf Hitler played ruthlessly on the popular desire for peace in France and Britain and on their governments' dread of precipitating a blood-letting even more terrible than that of 1914-18. At the Munich conference in September 1938 Hitler had informed the British Prime Minister, Neville Chamberlain, that he too was a humanitarian and hated the thought of "little babies killed by gas bombs".

Chamberlain bought "peace for our time" at Munich, but at the cost of surrendering Czechoslovakia's Sudetenland to Germany. In Britain there was an almost universal feeling of relief. If war had come, it was expected to take the form of an immediate series of crushing air raids in which Britain's cities would be drenched with gas bombs. The gas mask, a morbid momento of the Western Front and a harbinger of a new kind of war against mass civilian populations, was one of the most potent symbols of the Munich crisis. Adults and children in Britain were issued with these objects, whose sinister snouts, smell of disinfectant and breathless, clammy grip provided a chilling intimation of horrors in store. Small-scale evacuations of women and children from Britain's cities were also undertaken by the government, a dry run for the mass evacuations which were to take place at the beginning of September 1939.

Relief at the Munich settlement quickly gave way to a revived sense of foreboding. The landmarks of daily life were increasingly over-shadowed by the preparations for conflict that characterized the twelve months between Chamberlain's first flight to Germany in mid-September 1938 and 3 September 1939, the sunny Sunday on which he broadcast to the nation that "we are now at war with Germany". The conflicting emotions felt by ordinary people during this sombre period in our history are reflected in the diaries and memories of a number of very different women observers. The routines of everyday life were now interrupted by the disquieting spectacle of gas masks being donned in suburban sitting rooms and trenches being dug in public parks. As war approached, the landscape of towns and cities was transformed by civil defence measures, and the changes were noticeable even in the depths of the countryside.

Shameful though it seemed in retrospect, the Munich settlement had secured a vital breathing space

— time in which to rearm and prepare for the worst. By the spring of 1939 most people were reconciled to the inevitability of war with Germany.

On 13 September 1938, Neville Chamberlain sent a telegram to Hitler proposing that he fly to Germany to try to find a peaceful solution to the crisis which had arisen over Germany's claim to the Czech Sudetenland, which contained a substantial German-speaking population.

On the 15th Chamberlain flew to Germany — at the age of sixty-nine it was his first trip in an aeroplane — and was greeted by Hitler on the steps of the Berghof, the Führer's mountain retreat in southern Bavaria. Chamberlain returned to London the next day and then flew back to Germany on the 22nd for more talks with Hitler at Godesberg on the Rhine. A final series of meetings began on 29 September when Hitler, Chamberlain, the Italian dictator Mussolini and the French Prime Minister Edouard Daladier assembled at Munich to decide the fate of Czechoslovakia. The Czechs were excluded. While their ministers waited nervously in an ante-room, the Sudetenland was ceded to Germany; Poland and Hungary also received several thousand square miles of Czech territory. At a stroke Czechoslovakia had become a truncated, defenceless territory in a central Europe dominated by Germany.

Chamberlain returned to a hero's welcome, but his triumph was to be short-lived. At the beginning of the crisis Miss Vivienne Hall, an office worker who lived with her mother in Putney, south London, confided her thoughts to her diary.

13 SEPTEMBER 1938. "NO WAR". The *Daily Mirror* printed in thick black type these happy words. Coming from a restless bed I encountered Margaret, who brought me the paper while our beloved Puck[1] carried

---

[1] The family dog.

the *Daily Express* to Auntie. This paper was not quite so certain and all the meaning in Hitler's speech was brought out menacingly. I felt less apprehensive, however. I visited the theatre[2] in the evening and found a lot of joking going on around me as to whether we should enter the theatre in peace and leave it at war. The little vibration of fear started again in my tummy but I enjoyed *She too was Young* and returned home through streets lined with newspaper boys — a rare harvest for them.

Incidents in Czech-Nazi territory are rife. The Sudetens are clamouring for their rights and martial law reigns in the disturbed areas.

16 SEPTEMBER 1938. "PREMIER'S FRIENDLY TALK WITH HITLER". I wonder! We read last night of the cheering welcome accorded to the Premier by thousands of Germans and the brighter outlook by all nations at the swift and dramatic step of Britain — and of the general strike of Czechs; of the Nazi refugees streaming into Germany; of the numbers of incidents here, there and everywhere and it was all too confusing for my simple brain — I can't pick out the truth from the newspapers — so much we are told in them is obviously make-believe and sensation-causing. This week seems to be never-ending and the constant reiteration that "the next 48 hours will decide" has become irritation. I almost feel that if it *must* be war it ought to start right away and let us get over the horror — and then I think of the four years of the last War

---

[2] She was a keen amateur actor and theatregoer.

(the War to end War; the War which would settle the nations once and for all; the War to which memorials clutter up the whole country — the War which was to teach us the folly of War!) and wonder.

I am given a report upon the ARP[3] precautions which might be taken in my Office. "So far," I type, "we have reached no definite decision in the matter" and I feel comforted to think that in the event of an air raid "no definite decision" as to any sort of protection has been reached for the hundreds of us working almost opposite the Bank of England and very near St Paul's Cathedral!

24 SEPTEMBER 1938. "CHAMBERLAIN RETURNING TODAY". The conversations seem to have collapsed. We were told yesterday that the talk to have taken place that morning was postponed — Chamberlain had written a note to Hitler stating that conversations could not be carried out unless a guarantee was given that there would be no troop movements by Germany while such conversations were taking place. There was no guarantee, apparently, and after a day of rumours it was heard that Mr Chamberlain and the entire British Staff would return today. The news bulletins last night were full of accounts of armies moving, slowly and relentlessly moving toward the frontiers everywhere. The nervous joking about it all has reappeared, young men in the office are laughing about uniforms and last games of tennis, soccer, rugger. I talked with a friend at home last night and

---

[3] Air Raid Precautions.

he, poor thing, was really frightened; he couldn't release his mind from the thoughts of his son going through far worse than the misery he endured in the last war.

On the day Chamberlain returned from Godesberg, Moyra Charlton, a twenty-year-old writer of children's books, was recording in her diary the impact of civil defence preparations in Takeley, the Essex village in which she lived with her parents.

24 SEPTEMBER 1938. A very busy and rather exhausting day. Made the beds with Julia and then went to church with Mum to help decorate for the harvest festival.

The afternoon was very business-like. Mum and Miss Kayser and I, with the nurse, went into Stortford and bought up half Boots for the seven First Aid posts in the village. We divided up the supplies and put them each in a biscuit tin. I am somewhat disturbed to find that I, being the only person in the village who has done a gas course, may be called upon to lecture!

We heard from Win today.[4] He has vanished with the regiment somewhere into the western desert. He sent me a very rough scrap of verse he had jotted down on his last night.

We heard the Premier's return to Croydon at 1 o'clock today, a very simple welcome for such a momentous return. He has been with the cabinet this evening and they meet again tomorrow morning.

[4] Her brother Wingate, serving with the 8th Hussars in Egypt.

I cannot believe we will be involved in another war, but if this crisis blows over we will have no peace. It is admitting that might is right that is so galling. Can God mean one man — one little tin god — to involve a continent in needless murder?

26 SEPTEMBER 1938. The Kinsman family drove me to Cavendish Square and I shopped till 11. Searched in vain for ARP Handbook no 2, which was sold out. . . .

We shopped in the afternoon and I drove home. Poor Mum had a cup of tea and rushed straight off to fetch Dad and go with him round the area to announce the First Aid lecture on Wednesday.

I walked up to Reid's in the rain and arranged to have a lesson about a car's insides tomorrow. I have bought a German dictionary and am starting to revive that dying flame.

Mum and Dad in very late for dinner. We tried to listen to Hitler but atmospherics were too bad. The telephone rang incessantly. Dad and I were off to a gas meeting at Hatfield Heath but at the last moment Dad was summoned to Dunmow for a meeting of wardens.[5] I went too.

Gas masks are being issued — Val and I are going to assemble them tomorrow, as lady volunteers were called for. Trenches are to be dug without delay and a census of the 800 odd inhabitants of Takeley (and of every village around) must be in by tomorrow evening.

27 SEPTEMBER 1938. The Whites called for me rather

[5] Air raid wardens.

7

early and we drove to Dunmow to the Maltings. Here, by 10 o'clock fifty odd women had congregated, but time crept on and no one appeared to enlighten us. We read headlines in the *Daily Mirror* and did a crossword, but no one came for three-quarters of an hour.

At last we set to work, on long trestle tables, assembling the masks. We were given a short demonstration on fitting them, but supervision and instruction were not very helpful and after doing about a thousand, we found that we had done them wrong, so we had to set to and adjust the rubber bands again — really a pig of a job. The assembling itself is hard on the hands and to start with we made heavy weather of it, but we got quite deft-fingered before the end.

We were at it for 7½ hours and had done over 10,000 before we left at 7.30, leaving 5,000 to be finished off by the evening volunteers. . . .

The progress of the Munich conference was followed closely by Vivienne Hall, whose see-sawing reactions to the "emergency" mirrored the mixed feelings which accompanied Chamberlain's all too brief moment of triumph.

1 OCTOBER 1938. "CHAMBERLAIN THE PEACE-MAKER". This ordinary-looking, old man has become a world hero. I feel as I felt when I had my appendix out, as though I had lost touch with things around me and that I can now pick up the threads of ordinary life again. I have remembered that I am going out to tea on Sunday; that I am going away to Saltdean on Tuesday for five days and that I have nothing ready; that *Snow White* is on at my local cinema and that I must see it

today or miss it (and that would never do). Funny how an emergency makes one realise one's responsibility to the world and when the emergency is at an end you forget the other world completely. The papers are reporting on murders and suicides again (the poor murderers have had a very thin time in the newspapers lately and must be feeling very left out!) — so we are slowly getting back to normal.

2 OCTOBER 1938. The papers yesterday were guarded in their remarks — the Sudetenland was being occupied, and Hitler is to lead an army in today or tomorrow (I forget which; this is disgraceful but I am actually not very interested now). The people are beginning to think about it all and, although the relief is immeasurable at the removal of the war threat, we all feel that we have behaved rather shabbily. I had tea with some friends of mine and watched their beautiful baby staggering about the room. I felt then that any shady trick was worth their happiness. Then, in the evening I listened to the Archbishop and his sermon didn't please me a bit. It seemed hypocritical to expect us to offer our prayers and sympathy to the Czechs when we were the cause of their misery. It's a stupid feeling, intense relief and thankfulness that I, personally, and all I care for, are safe and yet ashamed because we have bought our safety in a rather mean way.

Hitler was not to be bought off. In March 1939 Germany swallowed up the rest of Czechoslovakia. He then turned his attention north to the Baltic, the free port of Danzig and the

"Polish Corridor" which separated the bulk of Germany from its province of East Prussia. His demands that the Poles restore Danzig to Germany and permit the construction of road and rail links through the Corridor to East Prussia were turned down by the Polish government. On 23 March German troops occupied the city of Memel, on the border of East Prussia and Lithuania. Poland warned Hitler that any similar attempt to seize Danzig would mean war. A week later Britain and France declared that they would stand by Poland. The Western democracies were now bracing themselves for the outbreak of war.

Neither Britain nor France had the military means or will to honour their commitment to Poland, whose only potential guarantor was the Soviet Union. Throughout the summer of 1939 Britain, France and Germany angled for the support of Josef Stalin. On 21 August Hitler reeled in the prize, announcing that Germany and the Soviet Union were concluding a non-aggression pact; it was signed in Moscow two days later. On the following day Constance Miles, the fifty-eight-year-old wife of a retired army major and inhabitant of the village of Shere, near Guildford in Surrey, sat down to write a diary.

24 AUGUST 1939. Today the news is very bad. "We are," says Mr Chamberlain, "in imminent peril of war." Nobody seems to be happy any more. It was rather dreadful to see the people at Woolworths struggling round the curtain hook counter to buy apparatus for their dark draperies[6] — the girls serving were very stupid and rushed. I had great difficulty in getting some cold ham at the equally crowded grocers. Thronged with worried, wrinkled women, trying at the last moment to lay in things.

[6] For blackout precautions.

I went to tea at Miss Scott's, the head of the Red Cross Unit here, aged 70. Croquet was played, with true British phlegm. Muriel Murray and Dorothy Coppings both assured me with great earnestness that we were "bound to go to war for Poland". Our honour, etc. Miss Sandworth, a fine old woman, tells me she has a class of 30 Czech refugees who are learning English.

R. says, eating stewed apples with cream at dinner, he would not leave the house, as "refugees would smash everything to pieces".

Mrs R's daughter in Portsmouth heard tramping sailors and soldiers to and fro all night.

Have none of the happy conviction with which I went into the last war.

The diplomatic manoeuvring now gave way to military mobilization. On 29 August Hitler delivered an ultimatum to the Polish government with a twenty-four-hour deadline. As ultimata and diplomatic replies flashed back and forth across the wires, Vivienne Hall tried to cope with the tension of waiting for the storm to break.

30 AUGUST 1939. The City is now a mass of sandbags and cellophane paper is being pasted on large windows. "We are ready" says everyone, but if you ask "for what?" nobody knows. The whole point of this war business is that no-one knows exactly how horrible it will be, how many nations will ultimately be involved, how much gas warfare will be used, where the battlefield will be, how long it will last, how strong we or the rather problematical enemy are?

31 AUGUST 1939. We now wait in a tired, not-very-hopeful-but-perhaps-it-will-blow-over mood for any definite news which we feel must come some day. These messages which are flashing from Hitler to us and back seem to be holding things up and time, I suppose, is everything, but I can't help wondering what Poland thinks of it — after all it's Poland's country which is involved so how can we decide anything without her sanction or knowledge? Peculiar business altogether.

We heard yesterday from one of the boys who *were* in the Office that he has been digging for days, digging trenches for the soldiers and, having finished, they have been put to digging trenches in a nearby park for civilians — I noticed as I passed the Signals barracks yesterday that the "terriers"[7] there were stripped to the waist and shovelling sand into bags as hard as they could go, placing the full bags against their barracks. They all seem to be growing moustaches and are now very "tough"!

Long before the war the British government had made elaborate plans for the evacuation of mothers and children from areas threatened by bombing to designated reception areas in the country. It had been estimated that up to 3.5 million people would be moved, but only about half that number took advantage of the official scheme. Most of them had reached their destinations, amid conditions of varying chaos, by the evening of 3 September, the day Britain went to war with Germany. Many of the evacuated children were escorted to the reception areas by volunteers, among whom

[7] Territorial Army.

was twenty-six-year-old Josephine Pearce, who lived with her mother in Putney, south London. She had trained as a nurse and offered to help a teacher friend escort her schoolchildren from the East End.

It was still quite dark when Mildred and I left the hostel for her school. Gas masks were issued, food packs given out, labels written and pinned to each child. Most could not afford suitcases but had brown paper parcels. The parents were white-faced but calm at the parting.

We all walked to Mile End station where we would be told which train to take. Our children, even the very small ones, having started off so early were at first a bit dazed but as we neared the Underground some were quite excited for few had ever been in an Underground train, or any train for that matter. Down we all went, each group clinging to their own adult.

"Miss, where we going? Ain't our train ever comin'?" At last we were told to get into the next train. It was about 8.00 a.m. and all of us had been up since 3.30. The whole train was ours and we got in by groups.

"Where we going, Miss? What does grass look like?" Many an East End child of those days had never seen grass or butterflies.

"Miss, will we see cows? They make milk, don't they? Miss, will we see 'em make it?"

. . . All were tired and hungry, so out came the food parcels. We slept, we played and the little ones were solicitously comforted by their not much older brothers and sisters. Mildred and I, on seeing each other for a brief moment, burst out laughing. We did look a sight, weariness covered by smudges of soot! . . .

It was well after 8.00 p.m. when the train slowed to a stop in the middle of nowhere. Oh! how it rained. We were all out on a muddy path, soaking wet.

A man and some women were bent over a paper with only a torch for light. Much discussion was going on. Large coaches loomed before us but we had to stay in the rain whilst people argued about who wanted which child! They began to separate brother from sister but the tie of Cockney families was strong, nor would we permit this! I was no teacher but a nurse. These children had had enough. Cold, wet and hungry as they were I called out "Everyone into the buses."

Mildred and I got the head mistress to tell these people that they could allocate the children under cover in the village hall. Arrived at the hall, we found food and drink a great help. At last, after one and a half hours argument, they were sorted out, embussed and off into the dark.

Suddenly the buses came to a stop. It was pitch dark and still raining. Three children's names were called out and out of our sight they went. The door was again opened.

"Miss Offer, will you please join these children. You will live with them at the Manor."

Mildred was just getting off the bus when my name was called.

"Miss Pearce, you are going to lodge with the shepherd."

The shepherd's cottage was only lit by candles. The downstairs room was heated by the wash boiler and I

was left with one candle and "Good night, Miss." Did
I sleep? I do not know. At five thirty in the morning
there was movement downstairs. I was called to
breakfast. The shepherd's wife got it for me. She was
the cook at the Manor. Her husband had gone and
would be back at noon when I was to eat with him!

At eight o'clock I went to Mildred at the Manor and
rang the front door bell. A lofty butler opened the
door, looked me up and down and, on my explaining
who I was, the haughty reply came, "One does not
come to the front door. That is the servants' door over
there." I, the nurse, was outside the firmly shut door!
Mildred, the graduate, was billeted in the servants' hall
and her charges were on the other side of the baize
door! We could not help laughing!

On returning to my tiny stone shack, I found the
shepherd busy putting our dinner in the clothes boiler.
He just threw meat and unwashed vegetables into it
and when all was more or less cooked, the muddy
concoction was served.

**As war approached, Kate Phipps, a probationer nurse at
London's Westminster Hospital, found herself caught up in
last-minute preparations for the worst. Her diary reveals the
fretful mood of the period.**

28 AUGUST 1939. Tried to buy a stirrup pump for
Florence at the Army and Navy Stores, but they said
they would have none for at least six weeks . . . by
which time London no doubt would be burnt out!
Westminster Hosp. over staffed with VADs[8] today so

[8] Nurses of the Voluntary Aid Detachment.

had to sit at HQ sewing blackout curtains, a most depressing job. Why they can't machine them beats me . . . such a waste of time hemming them by hand!

29 AUGUST 1939. They are starting up a first aid treatment post at the Vincent Square Hospital so perhaps I'll go there. The babies have been evacuated and there is a great discussion going on as to whether casualties are to be decontaminated from mustard gas in the chapel or the mortuary! I should have thought there would be no question that the mortuary with its concrete floors would be best. The chapel eminently more suited to the dead! I said so and two of our members were shocked. Tempers are getting a bit edgy! They also mentioned (and this is good common sense) that golf balls make excellent hard pads when wrapped, to stop bleeding. So when I finally escaped from the curtain making I went to Woolworths and bought four!

The arrival of the blackout proved a shock.

2 SEPTEMBER 1939. Last night I went to the pictures, and when I came out I feared for the moment I had gone blind for it was nearly pitch dark, not a street lamp as far as I could see, and no lighted windows, except for one and there was a small crowd outside that and people saying "You'll get us all killed" and a voice of Authority saying "Put out that light". The only bright thing was the tiny coloured crosses on the traffic lights. Cars had only side lights and some had blue covers over their headlamps.

This morning I noticed that the police are decked out in steel helmets. Sauntering toward Victoria I met a woman carrying a suitcase, who asked me to direct her to the station, so I walked part of the way with her. To my surprise she told me she was a German who was trying to get home. She had worked in England for some years and had two sons in the German Army. She became very upset when the ticket office would hold out no hopes of her getting a boat, she thought she might get torn to pieces here if war broke out! I assured her that would not be the case, and left her inquiring for vessels going to Denmark, Norway or even Russia. I advised against Russia! Poor thing I was glad to have been able to do her this very slight service, even though she may well be tomorrow's enemy . . . it's Hitler and his stormtroopers who need wiping off the face of the map . . . for the good of the German people as well as the rest of the world.

Was amused to see a gang of police recruits (perhaps cohort would be a more tactful word here) marching into a police station. All kinds of clothes showing the varied class of person now being recruited. Was also interested to note when passing the side end of Buckingham Palace that the sentries were in full battle dress, no longer sporting their regulation scarlet with busby.

At dawn on 1 September German troops moved into Poland and within hours bombs were falling on Warsaw. In Shere the news was received with disbelief by Constance Miles.

2 SEPTEMBER 1939. A peaceful hush lies over all

England. I sit at five minutes to nine in the stuffiest of rooms, stuffy because it is so hot, as we have had to carefully draw our dark brown curtains across the windows, as the blackout is strictly enforced.

Dr S. came to see E. last night and said: "Oh, I've had a jolly day finishing up with sacking the cook. I found that she had been calling the Austrian house-maid 'You dirty German!', so I said 'You'll pack up your things NOW and go.' So that's that."...

Warsaw has been bombed six times today. I was looking at Madame Curie's book in which she speaks of walking out from Warsaw by the sandbanks of the fascinating river Vistula which she loved so much, she knows not why. Truly for the English now it is as if the Vistula flowed down Oxford Street, as one paper remarked.

The almost unbearable tension was finally broken by the declaration of war on Sunday, 3 September. At 11.15 am Constance Miles had listened to Neville Chamberlain's broadcast to the nation. Soon afterwards she was overtaken by a flurry of alarm over evacuees and blackout precautions.

3 SEPTEMBER 1939. *Sunday, Outbreak of War* The Prime Minister in the most delightfully English voice told us just after eleven that we were at War.

It seems incredible! As I write, the sad day has gone by. The evening sun is glowing on the garden, and Edie's border shows her African and French marigolds still beautifully fresh and golden.

Early this morning Madge reported that news had come from London and that Compulsory Billeting must begin at *once*. She asked me to go and watch over a tearful neighbour, an old widow, solitary in a large house, frightened of what might be coming to her.

R. and I went in a hurry to the loft; he said that soldiers might be billeted there comfortably. "*Who* is to move the billiard table?"

"Easily done," was the calm reply.

I put up the black curtains.

The maid returned from Wales by night mail train. All excitement over the journey. "I sat by a soldier and he gave me his orange. And whatever do you think, Madam?"

"I don't know I'm sure."

"He told us he was born in Haverfordwest!" She beams all over, it's her own town.

How one longs for all this NOT to have happened at this deceiving time of year! In no time the autumn winds will be howling and sobbing and moaning about, and we shall be darkening windows early. . . . Aeroplanes drone by all day long, all night long.

My neighbour, Mrs F., says a blazing light comes from my window. This is terrible! I thought it was perfectly screened. E. is going round to gaze tonight. I have a baby bulb above my head, tiny, so that I just can read. I think it must be the moon on the glass.

The King spoke on the radio, curiously slow and sad and with much lack of vitality. Better far that the Queen had spoken. I hope they will soon get them out of their London Palace.

Neville Chamberlain's speech was followed almost immediately by the first air raid warning of the war. Gwladys

Cox, a middle-aged housewife in north London, recorded her reactions.

SUNDAY, 3 SEPTEMBER 1939. Soon after breakfast, realizing that war was imminent, we went down to the basement cellar below this block, which the tobacconist has given us permission to use as a shelter, it being part of his premises, and placed there deck chairs, rugs, candles and matches. After that, being so fine and sunny, after a storm in the night, we took a stroll. While watching the barrage balloon in the cricket field. Mr Palmer, the Manager of Gow's fish shop in the Finchley Road, with whom we have dealt for so long, and his wife came along. They were insistent that we should leave town, the sooner the better, but we told them we were going to stick it out if we possibly could.

On returning home, we turned on the wireless and heard there was to be "an important announcement" by the Prime Minister at 11.15 am. So, with bated breath — the whole world was on tiptoe of expectancy this morning — we settled ourselves in the sitting room and listened to Mr Chamberlain's broadcast. He announced that, as there had been no reply by 11 am to our ultimatum we, as a nation, were at war with Germany.

I shall never forget the thrill of his closing words:-
"Now, may God bless you all. May he defend the right. It is the evil things we shall be fighting against — brute force, bad faith, injustice, oppression and persecution and against them I am certain that the right will prevail." Mr Chamberlain's speech was

followed by the playing of "God Save the King" for which I rose and remained standing until it was finished. Then almost immediately, to our unspeakable astonishment, the air-raid sirens sounded.

Quickly turning off the gas at the main, catching Bob[9] and shutting him in his basket, grabbing our gas-masks, we struggled down the several flights of stairs to the street, some yards along the pavement, down the area steps, along the dark winding passages, to our shelter. My knees were knocking together with weakness. While I stifled a strong desire to be sick, I was not exactly afraid, but nervous that I should be afraid; startled and bewildered, glimpsing dimly that already all my known world was toppling about my ears; and, behind all the mixed feelings was one of unreality, because the circumstances of this first alert held such an artificially dramatic element — as if the curtain having rung down on Peace, War-planes, which had been awaiting their cue in the wings, suddenly swooped into view before the footlights.

I remained in the shelter about half an hour gazing at the cobwebs, while Ralph[10] reconnoitred outside. When the all-clear sounded, we came upstairs to make preparations for Sunday Dinner. Later, we heard that the alert had been sounded for "an unidentified aircraft".

I spent the rest of the day "stripping" the window panes with gummed paper, against bomb blast, improving the blackout, and putting away unnecessary

[9] The cat.
[10] Her husband.

knick-knacks. In circumstances like these, we own far too many possessions!

Kate Phipps went to church on the morning of 3 September and was caught up in the febrile atmosphere of the first few minutes of the war. Later in the war she recalled that day.

I was sent to St Michael's, Chester Square, where it was announced that the service would be an informal one, that the Vicar was in the basement with a radio and would come and let us know when any message came through from the Prime Minister. Well, up he came and said "England is now at war with Germany . . . let us pray." But we never got far with that prayer. There was something in the distance, a most peculiar and sinister sound, the wail of sirens. I had never heard them before and was duly shocked. Nearer and nearer it came, as the fluctuating vibrations hit us like wailing banshees.

"That must be the result of an air raid warning red", I thought as I got to my feet and left the church. "Would there be time to get back to my post[11] in Soho," I asked a woman transport driver parked at the entrance to the square.

"Oh, no, it's a raid and the orders are for everyone to go to the trenches."

Well, I knew where those trenches were, I had seen them being dug, so I stood at the corner like a traffic cop holding out my hand and saying, "This way to the trenches, madam" and feeling absolutely idiotic and

[11] First aid post.

with my knees, I don't mind acknowledging, wobbling under me.

A warden appeared from somewhere, and as the stream of people from church now knew where to go, it seemed no longer my business, so I went down myself into a rather nice trench with seating and even a small Elsan toilet! Everyone looked rather grim, but there was no panic and people started talking in quiet tones to their next-door neighbours. One elderly woman started to cry quietly, but Mrs B.[12] gave her some smelling salts and she brightened up. I produced a crossword puzzle from my Sunday paper, but nobody seemed to want to try it! I think that knitting may be the answer to these interruptions to our day in future. Then after a short while the all clear went and the warden said we could leave. I had left my coat in the church and went back and claimed it from an efficient sidesman who had everyone's things stacked in the vestry! Mrs B. invited me over to her flat for a sherry.

I had to be back by 2 pm and found everyone very cross. They had sat in their shelter for ages because they had failed to hear the all clear, so the rest of the day was rather grim, until some of us went into a doctor's office and listened to the nine o'clock news and heard a replay of Chamberlain's speech to the nation. Then the doctor brought out a bottle of champagne and we drank to the downfall of Hitler and all his works.

The idea then came to me that I might just as well take a regular nurse's training and really become

[12] One of Kate Phipps' colleagues.

proficient at the job, instead of being an amateur at the end of the war and having nothing to show for it. I asked the doctor and he said it was a sensible idea, but that it might be difficult as I was older than the normal probationer. I said, "To hell with age, there's a war on", and everyone laughed!

CHAPTER
TWO

Under Fire

THE STORM BREAKS

The first air raid warning of the war had been a false alarm, and it set the tone for the ensuing eight months of "Phoney War" in which an uneasy calm settled over Western Europe as the autumn rains and fogs rolled in off the Atlantic.

Throughout the bitterly cold winter the 150,000 men of the British Expeditionary Force in France listened to lectures about "Why We Are Fighting" and wondered why they weren't. The RAF dropped pamphlets rather than bombs on Germany. In the early months of the war British civilians groping their way through the blackout were often in greater physical danger than their compatriots in the forces.

The government adopted the less than inspiring slogan "Business As Usual". Rationing was introduced in January 1940. A steady stream of evacuees returned to their homes. The national mood combined frustration over increasing amounts of "red tape" with apprehension about the future. As Gwladys Cox wrote three weeks into the conflict, "isn't this a queer war?"

The Phoney War came to an end on 18 April 1940 when, without warning, Germany invaded Denmark and Norway. On 10 May, the day that Winston Churchill replaced Neville Chamberlain as Prime Minister, Hitler launched an offensive in the west. In the north his Army Group B advanced into Holland; to the south Army Group A thrust through the wooded, hilly country of the Ardennes. Outflanking the Maginot Line, the French fortification system on the Franco-German border, the armoured spearheads of Army Group A crossed the River Meuse on 13 May and then swung north to trap huge numbers of French and British troops in northern France and Belgium. Although it was not immediately clear, by 13 May the Western Allies had already lost the Battle of France.

In England rumours were flying, as Kate Phipps noted in her diary.

12 MAY 1940. Well, W and O[1] have gone, and all sorts of rumours are flying about. We all went into Whitby to see them off yesterday and were surprised to find barriers across the road where the old toll bar used to be, and the soldiers were noting car numbers and the number of passengers. There were soldiers guarding the stations at both S and W (against invasion from the sea or parachutists one just doesn't know!). There is a

---

[1] Two servicemen friends.

tale going about that spies are being dropped behind our lines in France dressed as nuns, so of course the people at Sneaton Castle[2] are now highly suspect! How silly can one get!

Mr Seaton Gray is supposed to have seen an enemy plane come in during a sea fret recently which on arriving at the Hotel Metropole (flying very low!) suddenly rose perpendicularly into the air to avoid that horror! So now Whitby thinks Hitler really has a secret weapon. Really!

I had forgotten till I got to church this morning that it was Whitsunday. Coming out someone spotted a submarine at sea and we watched it in turn through somebody's field glasses. We stood on a flat tombstone to see better, and I couldn't help thinking of History. Women of other times had looked out to sea, while their men guarded the coast watching for the invaders . . . Saxons, Danes, Vikings, Jutes. . . . Some of these invaders had come and stayed . . . we in fact are their descendents. What's going to happen this time?

I said to Mrs Russell, "It's a wonderful year for primrose and forgetmenots."

"That's something Hitler can't take from us," she replied . . . but I am beginning to wonder!

At the outbreak of war Moyra Charlton joined the First Aid Nursing Yeomanry (FANY) as a driver, and for the first six months of the war drove an ambulance for Colchester Military Hospital. She volunteered for overseas service and in April 1940 was one of seventy drivers sent to France as No. 3 Ambulance/Car Company. Landing at Le Havre, they

---

[2] A girls' school run by Anglican nuns.

proceeded to Dieppe, where Charlton was quartered in the Hotel Richmond. Initially her diary reflects a quasi-holiday atmosphere in which the war seemed a long way off, although the news from Scandinavia was worrying.

9 APRIL 1940. We have just come in from a café where we had coffee and croissants and heard the news in French. It confirmed rumours of the morning — that Norway has been bombarded and is now at war with Germany, and that Hitler has either invaded, or is about to invade Denmark. All Europe seems to be going up like a great bonfire.

But surely the northern countries could have seen it coming when Finland was attacked? If only they had stood together then. And now — what? Holland and Belgium are in a terrible flap of course. I wonder what will happen?

In the evening the thirty drivers who take over the ambulances this week were read out and neither Claridge nor I were on it. We both felt slightly offended. I suppose we look too flippant! She is mess orderly, which includes washing-up, for the week. I have come off better as I am house-louse to the Richmond Hotel. Today I swept all the landings and stairs (four storeys), the hall and two downstairs rooms and found time to go out and have coffee with Esme at 11.

Had the whole afternoon off. Wandered round the shops, bought hairpins and oddments and practised my French. This place is full of what Mum would call "little men" or "little women round the corner" who will sew and wash and cobble and do anything for one.

Soon Moyra Charlton stopped scrubbing floors as her
contribution to the war effort, and got rather dirtier dealing
with ambulance engines. "We maintained hard in the
garage," she wrote on 29 April, "lying underneath the
vehicles scrubbing, tightening bolts, playing about with oil
and getting hot and sweaty and filthy." Her off-duty moments
were spent cycling through the lush Normandy countryside.
But on 10 May the German Army launched its offensive in
the west, and a few days later approaching military disaster
was heralded by the arrival of a growing flood of refugees
fleeing the German advance.

17 MAY 1940. Today the town is crowded with refugees
from Belgium — cars loaded with the family and
luggage, with bicycles strapped on in front and
mattresses on the roof for protection against machine
gun fire. One had a Belgian flag flying bravely on its
bonnet. Most of these are the richer people, but even
so it is very tragic.

9.35. Had a bath at the YWCA and Esme, Pat and
I went to dinner at the little restaurant down the
road, the Rocher de Cancale. We had a grand dinner
for 20 fr., beginning with hors d'oeuvres and ending
with gruyère and cherries. During the meal, one by
one, Belgian refugee families came in. These families,
with small tired little children, a nurse, a pet Scottie,
the elderly fat *grandmère*, were so charming-looking.
They were people like us, used to the same sort of
surroundings, happy families, who had probably left a
chateau and animals and loved possessions, and all
because of that devil incarnate Hitler. God, I hate the
Germans for this more than anything else. With two
of the families were a naval officer and a young army

officer. He was extremely smart and very attractive and kind-looking, without being handsome. He was most interested in us and, in spite of his wife and family, we all fell for him on sight! After that the crude gallantries of the Tommies in the street seemed nauseating!

I saw two refugee cars today which looked as if they had been bombed, spattered with mud and dirt to the roof. Today the Germans swooped down without warning on one of the crowded frontier towns.

No wounded trains yet. They must be held up. There may be one in tonight.

19 MAY 1940. Last night we had our first taste of bombing!

After dinner I went down to the station with Harrison. We dodged under a few railings, as we had no permit, and there was a refugee train in. The people were crowded into carriages and cattle trucks, and the front trucks were riddled with machine gun bullets. They were all filthy but fairly cheerful. We went up the train handing out sandwiches and cigarettes, which were much appreciated. They waved as the train went out.

We had to be in by 10 so walked back with Mortimer, Woolf and Gleed. A cloudy, moonlight night and quite warm. The warning went before we got to the Richmond, and I was still fully dressed when the ominous thumping began. The bombs began to fall with reverberating thuds. The others all scrambled into their clothes and we turned out of the house and proceeded with dignity and apprehension to one of the trenches on the front.

Here we sat damply in the dark for close on two hours. Apparently there were two bombers, flying high, we gathered, though they sounded near enough. There was the droning sound increasing overhead, the whistle of the bomb and then the thud of the explosion, which shook the ground and sent blast and débris sprinkling above us. We secretly felt a bit windy to start with as we thought they were going for the Casino, but I believe the harbour was the attraction, and most of their eggs fell in the sea.

We had no defence at all, either aerial or ground, except some Scotsmen, who blasted off light-hearted rifle salvos just over our heads and devoted loquacious army wit to us in between. Soldiers' humour is unquenchable.

So we heard the ear-splitting crack of musketry and smelt powder and heard bombs dropping around, a baptism of fire for the "soldier ladies". But it is rather swinish to bomb an unprotected hospital town, crowded with refugees.

Today the town is fuller of refugees than ever. They are a poorer, rougher type now, in all sorts of queer old cars and vans, and hordes of young lads on bicycles.

There have been six warnings today — a record, I think. Two were very close together. After supper we went down to the sea to find out the meaning of continual thumps and found the minesweepers were exploding the magnetic mines which were dropped outside the harbour mouth yesterday. It was a red, windy sunset and groups were accumulating on the front to see the spectacle. We saw two go off — one a real whopper — a great forked sheet of water shooting into the sky. All Dieppe shook.

When we got back to the Richmond three more van loads of refugees arrived, dog-tired. A kindly soldier helped the women down and even held a tiny baby — the Tommy always to the rescue! Just as they had got out the warning blared out from l'Hotel de Ville overhead and they had to stagger and crowd and scramble to the nearest shelter. We were watching from our window and God, we felt angry!

On 21 May Moyra Charlton's unit joined a long trek south-west, away from the advancing Germans. On the 27th — the day the entrapped BEF started to be evacuated from Dunkirk — they arrived in Nantes. In her diary she noted that they had lived "a public life. Washing, eating, brushing our teeth, even sleeping, we are overlooked by groups of British, French, Belgian and Dutch soldiery, Zouaves and ruffianly refugees. We wash at cold taps in front of the main entrance and sleep in the ambulances. It is 'roughing it' with a vengeance and I have never felt more thoroughly filthy, but if we can stick it out and stay cheerful we may, so to speak, win our spurs."

From 31 May to 13 June the unit was stationed in La Baule, near St Nazaire.

8 JUNE 1940. We had early lunch and then went down to meet the train[3], which was about half an hour late.

---

[3] There were 13 British ambulance trains in France, converted from conventional rolling stock and ferried across the Channel. Staffed by three medical officers, QAIMNS (Queen Alexandra's Imperial Military Nursing Service) sisters and forty RAMC orderlies, they could accommodate more than three hundred patients.

It was a French one. There is a horrid fascination about an ambulance train coming in; it snorts in slowly and one sees orderlies at the doors and, through the windows, men lying down. The engine stops and steams in the noon-day sun and there is a few minutes' pause; then the walking wounded begin to appear, hobbling and helping each other along — bandaged heads, arms in slings, dirty and hot in their tin hats and battledress in the sweltering heat. That is the worst time for us, while waiting in line to load up with nothing to do but watch and think. One feels sick and cold with apprehension. The rest of it — negotiating the rails and the platforms, seeing to the loading up and to doors and the step, and trying to avoid bumps all the way to the Casino[4], is a full time job.

One is so scared of recognising, in one of the dirty, haggard, unshaven faces, somebody who is a friend. Elizabeth Horn's brother is fighting on the Somme. Thank God Win is in Trans-Jordan.

A few days later she sailed from St Malo for England on board the *Princess Astrid*, a Belgian ship acting as a British troopship.

14 JUNE 1940. 11.30 am

We have just left France. We were conveyed by RASC lorries from stations to docks and went on board.

It is a glorious morning. The khaki troops against

---

[4] The base hospital was housed in the Casino.

the grey background of the ship are typical of the sober tones of modern war. We moved slowly, and with some manoeuvring, out of the narrow harbour mouth and an accordion played and the troops sang "Somewhere in France with You". Our throats felt lumpy and we were thoroughly fed up that we were leaving when there was still work to be done, after all our high hopes of two months ago.

Shortly after the outbreak of war Josephine Pearce had become engaged to a pilot officer in the RAF and joined the Civil Nursing Reserve, a voluntary organization of trained assistant nurses now augmented by Red Cross and St John Ambulance nurses. She recalls: "I found myself on a goods train in a siding at Goodmayes in Essex. We scrubbed and turned this into an ambulance train. . . . Our days were boring — we scrubbed, played cards and drilled rather a lot".

Her next move was to join the Voluntary Front Line Surgical Unit, founded in World War I by the redoubtable Mary Spears and funded in World War II by Lady Hadfield. The unit arrived in France in February 1940 and operated with a French commanding officer, a British "Directrice" (Mary Spears), and French and British staff. In March Pearce, who had dual French and British nationality, joined the unit, which was designated Field Ambulance Unit 228 and based in a convent in Alsace-Lorraine. She had not been there long when, she wrote later, she received tragic personal news.

A letter awaited me from Mrs Bidie. "So sorry to hear of John's death, my dear."

I had not had news of my fiancé for some time. This was a terrible shock. I had never received notification.

The nuns heard of my news and arranged for a

special Mass to be said early one morning, and when I arrived, there, kneeling at a side altar in this vast Chapel were nurses and MTC drivers, some soldiers, young doctors and Dr Gosset himself. All were of various beliefs. That is a deeply stored memory.

Unaware of the military disaster unfolding to the north, the Spears Hadfield unit did its best to treat the stream of hungry, wounded and exhausted French troops who passed through the sector, all the while waiting in vain for the British Army and Royal Air Force to arrive. But it was the Germans who arrived first.

What was happening in the sky? To our amazement hundreds of parachutes were falling. Then one of our young doctors called out *"Ce sont des hommes! Des Boches"*. They dropped mostly into the forest of Senart and also into fields. This was something new and terrible. Some of our French officers took one or two of us to nearby fields and taught us how to use revolvers.

We had recently received a few wounded Germans, and among them a Colonel who needed a blood transfusion to save his life. A French orderly generously offered his blood and Dr Bernard was about to give the transfusion when the German said, "I would rather die than have one drop of French blood", so nothing could be done for him and he died.

The medical unit was now on the move, although in the prevailing confusion no one knew exactly where the Germans were or what had happened to the Allied forces.

35

We seemed to be on our way back to Paris; we had no notion of where we were to set up hospital nor had we the slightest idea that the great retreat had begun and that we would be on the move until we reached England.

At "Maison Blanche", near Châlons, we drew a blank. Our official title in the Army was Ambulance Unit 228 but no one there had heard of us. We had been redirected to spend the night at Châlons, but there we were told to proceed to a new destination, but when we got there there was not a soul to be seen. What a war!

The German parachutists were continually doing their work rushing through the villages on their bicycles and calling out to the villagers "Get out, the Germans are coming." So the roads got more and more congested. No army could have moved against the enemy. Our drivers would often have to drive off the roads over the fields to avoid being machine gunned by the German planes straffing these desperate and bewildered old men and women, their furniture piled on handcarts. I remember seeing one old granny sitting on the top with a small dead baby in her arms.

We were now in the land where Champagne is made. While in that territory we were at times hungry. Food was getting difficult to obtain but not Champagne!

There is a third distilling, producing a cheap flat wine which is delicious but only drunk in the area, costing in those days about a penny a bottle. This we imbibed on empty stomachs until our little soldier cook turned up trumps. He produced eggs and cooked wonderful omelettes. We asked no questions. He produced food and we ate it. After all, he had been an expert burglar.

The next night the unit was billeted in a village. . . . We were awakened at a very early hour by movement in the house and strange sounds emanating from the chicken runs. We opened the door and found Monsieur and Madame carrying a precious swansdown mattress out to the garden and splitting it open among the hens. "Better the hens than the Boche," said Madame.

We went to the Mess for coffee and found that it was all being packed up. Dr Gosset asked for four nurses for the Brie Cheese depot at Guigny Railway station. If you have never scrubbed out a Brie Cheese factory to turn it into a dressing station, then I strongly advise you not to.

We had one satisfaction at Guigny. We had placed arrows leading from the main road through the loop road and back to the main road, intended to direct our wounded whom we never received. Three doctors and some orderlies were still there when the Germans passed along the main road and with Teutonic thoroughness they followed the arrows off the main road, round and back again causing a confused tangle of cursing Germans stuck in their vehicles, prevented by their own men from moving on. During this time our remaining officers crept away under a hedge, across fields and caught us up at Amance.

We were running out of petrol and now began the nightmare of syphoning it from one car or truck and squeezing ourselves into the other cars, abandoning those with no fuel.

Paris was now overrun and on the 16th June the French Army laid down its arms, but we did not as yet know this. Mrs Spears had found General Requin[5] and told him that if France made peace she must get us nurses home. . . .

We were now a very ragged convoy on our way to the Auvergne. The awful irony of it all was that the weather was wonderful, the sun shone on buttercups and daisies in the fields. As we were winding our way up the mountain roads to get away from the streams of refugees we saw a tiny glimpse of the real old spirit of France. We came out of the forests on to a vast plain. An old stone bridge crossed a stream, but, just before we reached this there was a big tree laid purposefully across the road. There glaring at us was an old man and a young lad. They had one gun and "they were defending France"! On looking at a little notebook I find, that, since leaving Lorraine on the 7th June we had been through the Departments of Moselle, Meuse and Aube, turned from Auxerre to Yonne, returning south crossing the Loire. This old man and the boy were the only barrier that stopped us. They examined our papers, then allowed us to continue our flight. That old man and boy were France.

In the pouring rain we found one of two Chateaux both called Epinasse. The French Air Force beat us to it and would not allow us even a barn. We heard Dr Gosset at Mrs Spears' car in the night and some of us

[5] Commander of the French Fourth Army.

were near enough to hear part of the conversation. "Almost all the British units have left France."

At this point French and British medical staff parted company. One of the French doctors and some of the medical students felt it was their responsibility to continue caring for the wounded. Josephine Pearce felt that her duty lay more with England than with France, and hoped to leave from Bordeaux — in any case, her dual nationality could have endangered the unit, for now that the French had surrendered the British were "the enemy". The French people, too, were often hostile, believing that the British forces had let them down.

On a road lined with poplar trees we saw a French Red Cross convoy and they syphoned off some petrol for us from their cars. Someone said Bordeaux was closed but we did reach it. The people were very hostile to us. The Consulate staff had all left except two young men and Lord Mellish Graham, military attaché. All were burning papers.

After numerous delays we reached Arcachon in blinding rain and thunder and lightning. We found all the pleasure-loving rich living their lives oblivious of war. A beautiful restaurant among trees served us with slices of roast beef, ham etc. We were so empty and heaven was on plates before us. We never ate it after all for a Royal Navy petty officer hurried up saying we must leave at once as there was a ship. At the harbour we waited on the jetty for two hours thinking of twenty-six plates of food left untouched. All was cancelled and we must return the next day.

At 3.30 am we were back at the jetty. Two sardine

boats and a naval launch took us on board. . . .
Suddenly we were in the hands of the Navy. They gave us
pillows and white blankets. *Matelots* were feeding us two-
hourly with hot soup. This was HMS *Galatea*. We were
taken to St Jean de Luz next and hauled aboard the *Etric*,
the last British ship to leave France. We took ten days to
zig-zag to England. . . . On 26 June we arrived at
Plymouth, all our lovely equipment lost in France.

While Moyra Charlton and Josephine Pearce were coping
with the chaotic conditions in a France on the verge of
humiliating defeat, the Royal Navy launched Operation
Dynamo, the evacuation of the Allied troops trapped inside
the defensive perimeter at Dunkirk. Between 27 May and
4 June the Royal Navy and an armada of "little ships"
plucked 338,000 British, Belgian and French troops from the
beaches around Dunkirk while overhead a furious battle for
air superiority raged between the Royal Air Force and the
Luftwaffe. For some weeks afterwards further lost and
exhausted groups of men were taken off at various ports
along the north and west coasts. All the British Expeditionary
Force's heavy equipment was abandoned in France.

Waiting to receive the defeated BEF in England was
another army, made up of thousands of volunteers who fed
and watered the weary troops and provided fresh clothes for
those who had nothing more than the grime-caked, oil-
sodden battledress (if any) in which they had sailed from
France. The results were sometimes surreal as Kentish
railway stations became congested with swarthy French
poilus[6] crammed into cricket whites and club blazers, but the
volunteers worked wonders, not least the indefatigable members of the Women's Voluntary Service (WVS).

[6] Nickname for French soldiers coined in World War I.

Mrs I. Phillips recalls the final stage of WVS operations in those hot, hectic days of June 1940.

For ten days or so our local WVS had been taking an active part in caring for the troops passing through our town and visiting a hospital nearby. These wounded were composed of men from British, French and Belgian units, and those of us who could speak a certain amount of French were needed there.

One morning the telephone rang very early. This time, it appeared the men were to be got out of Kent and sent as far away as possible. It was thought that there might be the danger of air-raids now that the Germans were in possession of all the French ports. Only those who had to be operated upon immediately or were really too bad to move were to be left behind. An enquiry had come through from somewhere to know if it was possible for us to feed and refresh these men while they were being transferred from bus to train, which would take a long time.

It was a glorious June morning when I set out, for we were in the middle of an early summer heat wave, but for once this was no blessing as later in the day, as on subsequent days, the heat blazed down on that station platform and on the waiting train, and added greatly to the men's discomfort.

When I arrived I found that a long wooden table had been found to act as a buffet to hold drinks, cups, saucers, etc., and the bookstall had produced a trestle table for washing up utensils. One or two of the organisers had arrived and were busy running backwards and forwards carrying crockery, producing teacloths and dishcloths, tin pails and kettles, while others drove up in cars laden with bottles of soft drinks, enormous slabs of cake, chocolate and cigarettes in abundance and tins of biscuits. I was set to work immediately on the slabs of cake which had to be cut up into pieces. Many of the local public houses had been most generous in supplying crockery and trays for our use and tobacconists and confectioners willingly handed over most of their stocks.

Besides ourselves there were the Sister in charge of the train, and two nurses with her, some of the staff of both the First Aid posts in our area, ambulance men and stretcher bearers. There was also a man in charge of the loading of the train. The stretcher bearers were volunteers, mostly drawn from the local shops and businesses, and they had had very little practice, but the very greatest credit is due to them for their gentle and sympathetic handling of the patients, and the agility with which they performed their task. One would have thought the whole experience was one which happened to them every day of their lives.

The first day there were a lot of walking cases, and the others were mostly injured limbs. The following days the cases were more serious, culminating on the last day with bad head and face wounds. In a way, this first day was the most difficult as we were all novices and had not yet got it running in the best way.

As soon as the first walking cases were off the buses they streamed up to the buffet asking for drinks. There were perhaps 30 to 40 of them, a great variety of uniforms, from the *Matelot* with the red pom-pom on his hat, to the smart blue of the RAF officers. They all mixed freely together and language seemed no bar to conversation. The proverbially English cup of tea seemed equally welcome to all nationalities, though we had obtained coffee in case it was needed. Perhaps they were a little nervous of that!

Soon the stretcher cases were being brought into the station and began to look anxiously round, first for a cigarette, which we instantly provided, and secondly for their own particular pal. This is where the man in charge of the loading up came in. In a perfectly wonderful manner he proceeded to sort out the men, instantly spotting an anxious face, and in the matter of a minute or two, the pal was found and laid beside his friend, or a reassurance given that as soon as the pal turned up he would be brought up. I remember one lad (he looked very young indeed as he lay there with a broken leg, in his RAF pilot officer's uniform) looking round in a very worried fashion. I asked him if I could do anything for him and he smiled and said he had lost his observer and had promised him he would stay beside him. I spoke to the man in authority and in a few minutes I turned round to meet a grin of happiness and saw that the observer, an even younger creature, with badly wounded hands, was lying happily beside his friend.

The loading of the train was a nightmare. By now it was terribly hot and the coaches were stifling. It was even worse for those on the bottom layer of racks as they had the misfortune to have two stretchers over them so that no air could circulate. As far as I know these conditions existed throughout all three journeys that the train made that week, as there was no other way it could be arranged in safety.

It was now time for us to board the train and take the men our refreshments. Many of the patients were unable to sit up, and the nurses were all busy, so we knelt down where we were and supported the men with one arm and fed them with drinks with the other, lying our trays on the floor while we did so, and so further impeding the stretcher bearers.

It was my first experience of badly wounded men, and I shall not forget the examples of courage and endurance that I saw during that time. The last day that week, a Saturday, was the worst, as the heat was even more intense. The cases that day were bad and I felt when I returned home at the end of it all that I would never smile again. But through the whole three days I never heard a word of complaint pass the lips of anyone, and whenever I have felt inclined to grumble or grouse I have thought of those men, put my fingers mentally on my lips and refrained.

At last the train was fully loaded, the last man had been fed, the last cigarette thrown in and then came the business of collecting the cups. This necessitated a frantic running up and down the train as the guard kept blowing his whistle and calling "Stand away there". With much creaking and groaning it finally drew out with arms still waving cups from the windows.

There remained nothing to do but Wash Up! This was a work of art as by then the water seemed to have run out. It was all done eventually, the tidying too, and well after lunch time I trailed wearily home feeling as if I were returning to another world.

The popular press had hailed the Dunkirk evacuations as a "miracle", but as Winston Churchill pointed out, wars are not won by evacuations. The reality of defeat was borne home powerfully to Nurse Kate Phipps, who was now working at the Emergency Medical Services Hospital established at Ashridge Manor in Hertfordshire. In a letter to a nursing friend in Canada, she recorded the arrival there of casualties from the shambles on the French beaches.

Well there we were on a lovely May day, with England's may hedges and chestnuts in full bloom enjoying the sunshine, and wondering when something was going to happen. The news from France had recently been confused, and when Churchill told the House (and the rest of us via the radio) that we were in for a bout of "blood sweat and tears", we realised something was very wrong. There was a lot of talk in the papers about panzers, and refugees and a Gap in the lines somewhere, but if your nurses are anything like ours you will know they don't pay too much attention to the news, if it isn't right on the doorstep! We were told to stand by for a convoy from France . . . and then suddenly it came.

There was a buzz of excitement, and a little "indigestion" or heartburn, for we had been practising for so long, and really did want to put up a good show. It was like standing on the stage waiting for the curtain to go up. One had perhaps over rehearsed and there was a horrid fear that it might suddenly turn into a quite different play, with a plot which was unfamiliar and lines which would have to be improvised. How right a hunch as it turned out!

Our staff nurse was a bit jittery, her fiancé was with the BEF, and some nasty rumours had been floating around to the effect that they were being evacuated under fire! But nobody knew anything definite, and half the tales we heard might be untrue. Sister McCabe entertained us while waiting with tales about the Irish rebellion (her mother was killed then) . . . she said "You must not be upset if the casualties smell a bit . . . I remember the stench of dried blood, just go ahead and clean them up, as if it was an everyday business, and make a bit of a joke, men like that". Then a car drove up.

Two officers got out, limping and were helped into ward 10. Then it dawned on us that indeed things were wrong . . . the officers were dirty, and untidy, one lacked a uniform coat, the other had a bloody sling on his arm. Surely after going thru the regular Army casualty routine someone would have cleaned them up! They looked as if they had come straight off the battlefield . . . but we were not a first field dressing post we were a base hospital . . . the terminal point in fact. What could have happened!

Then the green line buses arrived and started to unload, they were mostly stretcher cases, so the ARP men were kept busy. But they wore beards, and there were thomas splints stuck out at all angles and blood stained head bandages. They all looked so dirty and did they smell! I was glad Sister had warned us about the stench of dried blood. We wanted to smile a welcome but felt nearer crying.

What little uniform they had was in a bad state, we had to cut it off in most cases. "Down the seams nurse, it may have to be used again"! We found some of the wounds had field dressings still on that had stuck, and had to be soaked off. Their feet were in a bad state from marching and socks too had to be cut off. My scissors got so blunt in cutting through the heavy khaki, that in the end it was like sawing, but somehow we got them undressed. The men seemed dead tired, and we had to wash many asleep.

Pathetic little bits of equipment came in with the men, the odd gas mask, and a few tin hats. Out of forty men we have only been able to collect three rifles, eight gas masks and twenty tin hats, and men under fire as these have been will stick to their helmets whatever else goes! What can have happened we asked each other and the men. But they didn't know; said the Frenchies had let them down and the bloody panzers were everywhere. But an army making a planned withdrawal doesn't send its wounded home in that condition, neither do men abandon their equipment!

We stayed on duty till nearly midnight, and just before we went off one man with a head wound had a haemorrhage and had to be rushed off. His pillow was soaked with blood and I had to make up his bed in case he returned . . . (To my surprise I found him there next morning, these men are tough.) It took me a little while to go to sleep, in spite of being so tired, I could not help thinking of those wounded who had not been collected lying out in ditches or fields with no help at hand.

The Medical Supt (known as Pooh Bah) came with a fussy little army doc who said the men must stand to attention beside their beds when a doctor inspected! He started to make criticisms, but sister was quite equal to the occasion and he retired hastily! The men laughed and made rude noises when he was gone.

For older but no less redoubtable Englishwomen, there were alternatives to nursing. If France had been defeated, then Britain must be next. Gwladys Cox had already volunteered for ARP work in north London. And the fear of gas attack, the great horror of World War I, still loomed large, as is shown in the diary of Vere Hodgson, a middle-aged spinster who worked for a religious and philanthropic trust, the Greater World Association, with headquarters in London's Holland Park.

12 JULY 1940. Went to Gas Lecture in the evening. They passed round little bottles of some of the gases. I had a good sniff at Lewisite. It is definitely a very strong smell. I should say it is like Geraniums. Then the Lecturer broke a capsule of phosgene. You can call it Musty Hay, if you like. It certainly is like Decaying Vegetation. Mustard seemed to have a very definite smell — but I could not say what of.

18 JULY 1940. We had a lecture on incendiary bombs and then were taken out to do the practical! What a morning! It was pouring with rain.

The first act was the Stirrup pump. Having used this before I earned a VERY GOOD from the instructor.

Next the corrugated iron hut was closed up, and one by one we had to creep through a door and work our way on hands and knees through the smoke and with a fierce fire burning in the centre of the room! Towards the end we were asked to stand up, and when we were choked to get down again on the floor.

The next episode was the Bomb. The side of the hut was let down and a rough room created with the fire still going well in the centre. In the room was the Bomb. Some old furniture was spread around the room and sprinkled with petrol. It was all set on fire and we had to use the stirrup pump and cope with Bomb and fire at the same time.

THE BATTLE OF BRITAIN

When it became clear to Hitler that the British government had no intention of entertaining his peace overtures, he began to consider plans for a cross-Channel invasion codenamed Sealion. On 18 June Winston Churchill told the House of Commons, "The Battle of France is over. I expect that the Battle of Britain is about to begin."

Crucial to the success of Sealion was air control over the English Channel and south-east England, but barring Hitler's way were the squadrons of RAF Fighter Command, led by Air Chief Marshal Sir Hugh Dowding. In the front line were "The Few", the gallant young Hurricane and Spitfire pilots. Behind them were "The Many", the technical and logistic arms which kept them flying. Not least among them were those serving with the Women's Auxiliary Air Force, which had been formed in June 1939. By the outbreak of war the

WAAF numbered nearly eight thousand officers and air-women.

The first phase of the Battle of Britain began on 10 July 1940 as the Luftwaffe launched a series of probing attacks on Channel convoys and coastal targets, seeking out the weaknesses in Fighter Command's defences. Vital to these defences was the "Chain Home" (CH) system of radar stations strung along Britain's south-western, southern and eastern coastlines and from which reports were fed to Fighter Command Headquarters at Bentley Priory, Stanmore, in Middlesex.

Along with information from coastal and inland posts manned by the Observer Corps, the radar plots were passed through the "Filter Room" at Bentley Priory to the Operations Room, from which overall control of the unfolding battle was exercised.

Here aircraft tracks over the whole of Britain and the sea approaches were displayed, enabling Dowding and his senior commanders to gain a full picture of the Battle as WAAF plotters moved aircraft symbols across the chart with long rakes.

The information was then relayed to the relevant Fighter Group Operations Rooms and in turn to the Group's sector stations, where the Group Controller allocated interceptor squadrons which were then scrambled to meet the incoming aircraft.

On 30 July Hitler ordered Hermann Goering, the commander-in-chief of the Luftwaffe, to prepare "immediately and with the greatest haste . . . the great battle of the German Air Force against England".

In August the Battle intensified as the Luftwaffe focused its attacks on Fighter Command's sector airfields in the key area of the south-east controlled by Air Vice-Marshall Keith Park's 11 Group. At the same time it attempted to blind Fighter Command by destroying its "eyes" — the radar stations on the south coast.

In the front line on 18 August was the radar station at Poling, three miles east of Arundel in Sussex. Serving there as a radar operator was twenty-four-year-old Corporal Avis Hearn, who, at only four feet ten inches, was the smallest woman in the WAAF.

I was one of the first batch of WAAFs to train as a radar operator at Bawdsey, in Suffolk. In December 1939 we were posted to Poling. It was terribly "hush hush". The local people probably thought that our two tall radar masts — one for transmitting and one for receiving — were some kind of science fiction "death ray".

There was no accommodation for us at Poling station, and we were put up in very grand circumstances at Arundel Castle, with a suite of rooms and a butler waiting on us at meals. Conditions at Poling were fairly rough and ready. The radar operators were housed in little more than garden huts protected with a pile of sandbags. A new concrete bomb-proof building, with a curtain of blast walls, was being built for us, but we had not moved into it by the summer of 1940, although our telephone links had already been transferred there.

By mid-August we knew that our turn would come soon as the Luftwaffe had already attacked the radar stations at Rye, Pevensey and Ventnor. On Sunday the 18th we were due to go on duty at 1 pm. When we started, our screens quickly indicated a big raid building up over France. You could see the formations assembling before crossing the Channel.

Sergeant Blundell, who was in charge of our watch, ordered me over to the bomb-proof building to deal with the Chain Home (Low) transmissions from the neighbouring station at Truleigh Hill. The job of the CHL stations was to track low-level raiders trying to fly in under the "Chain Home" cover. Normally two WAAFs handled the CHL transmissions, one receiving the plots and the other passing them by telephone to the Filter Room at Bentley Priory. But we were short-handed, so I agreed to replace the WAAF who was there and operate singlehanded for an hour.

It was now about 1.30 pm. No sooner had I sat down in the Receiving Hut than Sergeant Blundell rang through to me, telling me to "duck" as raiders were approaching. I told him I couldn't leave my post as there was so much information coming in from the CHL station, so he said, "I'll leave it to you!"

Then the operator at Truleigh Hill came on the line, saying, "Poling! Poling! The last plot is right on top of you!" which I knew perfectly well as bombs were already falling on the station and I could hear the scream of the dive bombers as they swooped down. Bombs were exploding all round the building.

At this point a civilian burst into the room. I didn't have a clue who he was but, shouting above the din, I handed him the telephone receiver and told him to repeat everything I said. He could have been a spy for all I knew! Later I learnt that he was a Post Office engineer and that he had had a nervous breakdown after the raid.

At the other end of the line the plotter at Bentley

Priory was asking, "Are you all right? Are you all right?" In the meantime I crammed my tin hat on — it was the only time I ever wore it.

The next thing I knew was that the door had blown in and there was dust flying everywhere. The lines went dead and the telephone switchboard came alive, with all the lights popping and bells ringing. An officer appeared, telling us to get out as quickly as possible. Outside there was devastation and not a soul to be seen. Craters everywhere, the concrete aerial supports pitted by machine gun bullets and the top of one of the masts shorn away. The lorry which had brought us to Poling that morning was burning fiercely, and the officer's lovely Lagonda sports car was a gutted wreck. Our only defence was a Lewis gun manned by an Army detachment whose billet was a mass of flames. Later I was told that the Germans had dropped about 80 500lb bombs, of which half had hit the radar station.

On reflection, the arrival of the Post Office engineer probably saved my life. If he hadn't turned up, I might have been tempted to run for it. I wouldn't have stood a chance. . . . Outside the station we passed an ambulance and a fire engine, which had been held back at the gates because of the top secret nature of the radio equipment.

That afternoon I went to church at Arundel and fell down on my knees to thank God for deliverance. Then I walked over to the nearby golf course to see a downed German aircraft, a "Stuka" dive bomber. The soldiers guarding it lifted me up into the cockpit, which was caked in vomit. Later I heard that the "Stuka's" rear

gunner had died of his wounds. Ironically the dive
bomber was not one of our attackers but had been shot
down in the fight over the Fleet Air Arm station at
Ford. . . .

After the attack we were moved into a mobile radar
unit housed in two caravans, one to receive and one to
transmit, concealed in Angmering woods. In two days
we were back on the air and operating. On my first
watch we picked up another big raid, which was
broken up before it reached us. I must admit that I was
afraid this time — on the 18th I was so intent on my
task that I had no time to feel fear. I don't think
there's such a thing as a brave person. You don't feel
you're doing anything brave, you're just doing your
job.

**On 22 March 1941 Avis Hearn was decorated with the
Military Medal by King George VI at Buckingham Palace. By
the end of August 1940 the aerial battle over south-east
England was nearing its climax. In the fields and towns below
people watched the skies, flecked with the vapour trails of
duelling aircraft, and waited. Constance Miles wrote in her
diary.**

30 AUGUST 1940. Air raids this morning over Shere. I
sat with Nina in her coal cellar under the stairs. With
us was a tiny girl aged three called Shirley with her
mother from Portsmouth. It was wretched hearing the
child talk as the planes droned away.

"Mummy, they won't hurt us, will they? They did
bomb a lot last night, didn't they, Mummy? They are
coming back, Mummy!"

One would fear the effects more on older children, of course. Guns over London are firing as I write — ten o'clock.

Here is a true story I like. During a raid yesterday 92-year-old Mrs Turner was assisted from a train to a shelter in a London district.

On reaching the entrance she turned to the Warden and said: "An ancient Briton returns to her cave."

THE BLITZ

London and its citizens were now thrust into the front line. Hitler had expressly forbidden the bombing of the capital, fearing reprisals against Germany's cities. But on the night of 24-25 August several Heinkel bombers missed their designated targets and scattered bombs across the East End of London. The next night Bomber Command retaliated, despatching 81 Wellington bombers to raid Berlin. On 4 September Hitler promised a wildly cheering audience in Berlin that the Luftwaffe would now raze Britain's cities to the ground.

Late in the afternoon of Saturday, 7 September the Luftwaffe arrived in overwhelming force over London. A total of 348 bombers, escorted by 617 fighters, attacked the docks. As darkness fell more bombers arrived to add further high explosive and incendiaries to the inferno raging below in the close packed streets of the East End. The Blitz had begun.

Throughout the Blitz women played a vital role in Britain's civil defences, serving as firewomen in the Auxiliary Fire Service, ambulance drivers, despatch riders, nurses staffing First Aid posts and Air Raid Wardens.

At the local level, the key to the civil defence system was the Air Raid Warden's post — clearly marked and heavily sandbagged — which was not only the hub of activity but also provided the information which, when fed up through the chain of command, help to provide an overall picture of the situation during a raid.

At the height of the Blitz one Warden in every six was a woman. Barbara Nixon's beat was in a borough bordering the City of London. Here she describes her first "incident", the bureaucratic euphemism invented to describe every sort of disaster inflicted on the civilian population by an air raid.

It was a grey, damp afternoon in late September, ten days after the start of the air-blitz on London. I was bicycling along a shabby street in a district some miles from my own. The day alerts were so frequent that it was difficult to remember whether the last wailing of the siren had been the alert or the "all clear."

Suddenly, before I heard a sound, the shabby, ill-lit, five-storey building ahead of me swelled out like a child's balloon, or like a Walt Disney house having hiccups. I looked at it in astonishment, that bricks and mortar could stretch like rubber. At the point when it must burst, the glass fell out. It did not hurtle, it simply cracked and dropped out, allowing the straining building to deflate and return to normal. Almost instantaneously there was a crash and a double explosion in the street to my right. As the blast of air reached me I left my saddle and sailed through the air, heading for the area railings. The tin hat on my shoulder took the impact, and as I stood up I was mildly surprised to find that I was not hurt in the least. I had not heard any whistle of the bombs coming down, only the explosion, and now the sound of an aeroplane's engine starting up. I thought, "So it's true

— you don't hear the one that gets, or nearly gets, you."

For no reason except that one handbook had said so, I blew my whistle. An old lady appeared in her doorway and asked, "What was all that?" I told her it was a bomb, but she was stone-deaf and I had to abandon bawling for pantomime of a bomb exploding before she would agree to go into a surface shelter. After putting a dressing on some small cuts on a man's face, I turned back towards the site of the damage. I did not know the locality, but, again, the handbook said that when an alert sounded, a warden away from his home area should report to the nearest Post.

At four in the afternoon there would certainly be casualties. Now I would know whether I was going to be of any use as a warden or not. I had to go warily, as if I were crossing a minefield with only a rough sketch of the position of the mines — only the danger-spots were in myself. I was not let down lightly. In the middle of the street lay the remains of a baby. It had been blown clean through the window, and had burst on striking the roadway. To my intense relief, pitiful and horrible as it was, I was not nauseated, and found a torn piece of curtain in which to wrap it. Two HE bombs had fallen on the new flats, and a third on an equally new garage opposite. In all this grimy derelict area, they had struck the only decent habitations.

The CD[7] services arrived quickly. There was a large number of "white hats," but as far as one could see no

7 Civil Defence.

one person took charge, and there were no blue incident flags. I offered my services, and was thanked but given nothing to do, so busied myself finding blankets to cover the five or six mutilated bodies in the street. A small boy, aged about 13, had one leg torn off and was still conscious, though he gave no sign of any pain. In the garage a man was pinned under a capsized Thorneycroft lorry, and most of the side wall and roof were piled on top of that. The Heavy Rescue Squad brought ropes, and heaved and tugged at the immense lorry. They got the man out, unconscious, but alive. He looked like a terra-cotta statue, his face, his teeth, his hair, were all a uniform brick colour.

Eleven had been killed but a large number were badly injured — an old man staggered down supported by two girls holding a towel to his face; as we laid him on a stretcher the towel dropped, and his face was shockingly cut away by glass. It was astonishing that he had been able to walk down stairs. Three more stretcher cars and two ambulances arrived, but they had to park some distance away because of the débris. If they had been directed to approach from the western side they could have driven much closer. The wardens began to check up the flats. As I did not know the residents, or how many of them there ought to be, I could not help, and stayed below.

But by now the news had travelled, and women back from shopping, girls, and a few men from local factories, came running and scrambling over the débris in the street. "Where is Julie?" "Is my Mum all right?" I was besieged, but I could not help them. They shouted the names of their relatives and scanned the faces of the dusty, dishevelled survivors. Those who found that they had lost a relation seemed numbed by the shock and were quiet, whereas a woman who found her family intact promptly had hysterics. The sudden relief from an awful fear was more unnerving at the moment than the confirmation of the fear.

For others, their first experience of bombing was less searing, though perhaps more bizarre. On 14 September Joan Wildish was in the process of marrying a young clergyman, Christopher Veazey, when the sirens went.

You took my hand and lifted my veil to kiss me. It gave me so much confidence I did not feel frightened. We walked to the vestry and out into the Rectory garden. Then, while the planes were battling for a life and death struggle overhead, we stood quietly for our photographs to be taken. Suddenly, without warning, a German plane flew in low over the house and released a bomb — I shouted to the photographer who was under the black velvet cloth trying to take the photo, "Look out, he's dropping bombs!" The man just shouted back from under the cloth, "Never mind about the bomb — JUST SMILE!"

Following the first raid on 7 September, Londoners endured fifty-seven consecutive nights of bombing. They quickly became "Blitzwise", learning to adapt the everyday routines of life to the new rhythms imposed by the nightly arrival of the Luftwaffe and the destruction and disruption the bombers left behind them as they flew away. In a letter to her friend in Canada, Kate Phipps gave a visitor's view of London life and the camaraderie in the bomb shelters.

My most vivid memory is of sitting under a railway platform in a sort of subway wearing my ersatz tin hat. The passengers had all been bundled out of our train, and my main worry was would I miss my connection at the next station! You could hear the throb of the aircraft overhead, and bombs not too near, but the jerries evidently raced for home as the all clear soon went and we dashed for the train, and I made my connection by the skin of my teeth. I have this dated as *Sept 10th*, and a note that when I got into my second train it was packed with evacuees from the East End. An old grannie, a mother, four small children and a canary were in my carriage, and two men belonging to an aircraft factory (one of the old fashioned carriages that hold ten people at a squeeze). "My God" said grannie "I hope they get Hitler for this", but her daughter replied "You know Mum I think we're lucky; after all we had nothing to lose . . . look at all these nice homes and gardens smashed up, and our Nellie just paid off the hire purchase on the furniture, and they lost the lot . . . well we never did have anything did we."

I found Mappin and Webb's shelter fascinating. They are a very smart and expensive firm of jewellers, and I happened to be passing when the sirens went, and followed the crowd down a side alley. I noticed that one of the shop assistants fastened a thick wire grating over the windows before going to shelter and I asked him if it was to protect the glass. "Oh no" he said. "In case of looting." The cellars were most elegant and ancient; and full of shelves where the exclusive china, leather goods, silverware etc and the jewel safes were. One of the assistants told me that there are tunnels running under several shops which fetch up under a church. They date from the fifteenth or sixteenth centuries!

It was interesting to note the sudden change in "persona" (as the psychiatrists say) when the shop walkers put on wardens' tin hats and the rest of the uniform. From being rather suave servile shop employees they became people of importance and joked with the customers, and shepherded people in off the street.

On this occasion the staff even came round offering us cups of tea and boiled sweets! A young man sitting opposite me was composing music. He says he always does this in his spare time ("classical of course not jazz" he added).

The Blitz lasted from 7 September 1940 to mid-May 1941, during which time high explosives and incendiaries destroyed 220,000 of London's houses and rendered another 1.5 million either temporarily or permanently uninhabitable. On 1 October while she was sheltering in the cellar with her husband, Gwladys Cox's flat in West Hampstead became another Blitz statistic.

The bottom of our world has dropped out. Last night most of our home, together with the whole top floor of Symington Mansions, was destroyed by incendiary bombs.

Ralph, Bob and I are in Mrs Snepps' dining-room and once more we are settling down for the night, but in what different surroundings! Ralph in a big comfortable armchair, Bob in a small one, I on the settee. We are fully dressed, wrapped up in Mrs Snepps' eiderdowns. The guns are blazing away, an alert is on, and it is as noisy a night as any.

To go back to last night. Just as I had written the last words in my diary, there was a terrible crash quite close, to the east of us, making the building stagger. We sprang to our feet, dragged on overcoats, shut Bob in his basket and put out the lamps and stove. Almost immediately, the plunk, plunk of incendiary bombs was heard above, on OUR OWN ROOF! The sound was different to anything in the nature of a bomb I had heard before, almost soft, in comparison to the loud bangs and crashes to which we had become accustomed — firm, spaced, even, like the footfalls of some giant stepping mincingly over the tiles.

Ralph immediately rushed out and up the area steps and found an ARP warden extinguishing a blazing incendiary in the street. He then ran upstairs, and actually got into our flat. . . .

All was confusion now at the bottom of the area steps — Wardens and Firemen shouting at each other and giving contradictory orders. One Warden seemed annoyed we had left our cellar and ordered us back but we could not return as water was already pouring down from their fire-hoses above; another shouted at us, "Keep your torches down! Don't flash your torches! Can't you hear Jerry overhead?" (There was already a big blaze above us to guide Jerry!)

I pushed ahead grabbing at the iron railings of the area steps, and halfway up fell against Ralph.

"For God's sake, come quickly!" he exclaimed,

"The whole of the top storey is on fire!"

He took Bob, dragged me up the rest of the steps and we faltered along the pavement. We stumbled along blindly in the inky darkness over innumerable fire hoses, water swilling everywhere, our shoes wet through. How little did I think when I wrote, that serene June day, of the AFS[8] tank water shimmering in the sun, that it would first be used to flood our house!

We groped our way to the brick ARP street shelter at the top of Sumatra Road. Here, in the dark and cold, we found other occupants of Symington Mansions, including the Samuels and the Solomons. Mrs Samuels clutched Kitty in her basket. She had rushed up to get the cat with smoke pouring down the staircase. We all fell on each other's necks, like shipwrecked mariners meeting on a desert island.

The sights and sounds of the Blitz, a mixture of the surreal and the terrifying, were evocatively remembered in an account of a nightmarish journey through London by Dora Chicken, who was an ARP Deputy Controller in Southgate. This was a night spent away from the control room in the company of an airman, Flight Lieutenant Thomas Hart. Their evening began in a smart restaurant.

He chatted with animation while we ate, and then the band struck up "A Nightingale sang in Berkeley Square", and we danced and sang. I looked at the other dancers. How attractive they looked, and what a variety of uniforms — Dutch, Belgians, Norwegians,

[8] Auxiliary Fire Service.

Czechs, Poles and Free French. Many of the ladies wore uniform: others were wearing long dresses. Then the air raid warning wailed, and the restaurant manager announced that there was a shelter in the basement for those who wished to use it. Some left, but the band played on and many continued to eat and dance. We then heard the distant crackle of anti-aircraft fire. . . .

"They're dropping them in sticks of five now," said Tommy. "Let's get under the table — at least we'll be protected from falling plaster." He lifted the heavily starched white table-cloth, and pulled me under the table — other people doing the same. A tremendous explosion shook the entire building, and we heard the shattering of glass and falling plaster. The lights failed momentarily, and we could hear people coughing to clear the dust from their throats. . . .

The noisy guns and explosions eased, and a singer from the band began to croon Jerome Kern's "All the Things you Are".

"Let's practise for next Thursday's Mess party. I must get some new verses together", he said.

"Don't you dare sing any of those bawdy RAF songs here", I remonstrated in a low voice. "This is a respectable restaurant, and we'll want to come here again. I don't want to be black-balled."

"Well, let's compose some verses to the tune of 'My Bonnie lies over the Ocean' — nothing crude — just nicely suggestive", he instructed. "I've got the first verse, listen" — he sang very softly —

My father's a candlestick maker,

My mother she peddles in gin
My sister goes out in the evenings,
My God, how the money rolls in.

"Then we all sing the chorus, O.K.?" Our efforts, conducted in whispers, brought gusts of hearty laughter from under the table. Then a superior, starchy waiter, like a stuffed penguin, raised the cloth, looked down on us, his nostrils quivering, and said, "The danger seems to have passed for the moment, sir, will you take your coffee under or on top of the table?". . .

"Come on", he said, "Let me get you home to safety." He sped, like the wind, along Picadilly, dodging the fire engines and ambulances. The guns were now deafening. My heart was thudding as I saw a church on the right of us mushroom into the air with an ear-splitting explosion. We turned into Shaftesbury Avenue. Then, suddenly, I shouted, "Look out, Tommy. Watch it — brake."

The moon had gone behind a cloud, and we had only the light of the blazing buildings to help us. Tommy put his foot down hard on the brake. We stopped on the edge of a crater surrounded by fallen masonry. . . .

We were now out of the car and Tommy was measuring with his eye the distance between the wall and the edge of the crater. At that moment there was a deafening explosion, a blinding flash and a frightening rush of air. I covered my face with my hands, but like a rabbit mesmerised by a snake, the fascination of the horror compelled me to peer through my open fingers. Crouching and reeling backwards, I cried in anguish "Jesus Christ." This was not a profanity. It was a prayer and came from the very depths of my being. I was apalled and disgusted. A block of flats had been split from top to bottom. It looked like a doll's house with the front open. I could see, in the light of the flames, mirrors and pictures suspended drunkenly from the walls, and amazingly, some furniture remained as it was. I thought that my eyes were playing tricks, and that I was looking at the upright, headless body of a woman, but then I realised that it was merely a dressmaker's dummy on which a partly made dress was draped. Hanging hideously between floors, was a bed, its covers flapping eerily in the breeze. . . .

I had no idea of how to find Tommy, or, God forbid, whether he had been a victim of this last explosion from which I had recoiled as it threatened to take my breath away.

I was extremely cold for I had lost my warm woollen evening cape, and, as was the fashion of the day, my dress was strapless. A Civil Defence man shouted at me — "Hey you — get under cover somewhere, you silly little bitch."

"Shelter — where?" I answered sardonically.

Being alone, he must have thought I was a streetwalker. How ridiculous, clad like this, and crawling through dust and sharp stones. A drunken serviceman reeled towards me. He grabbed my bare shoulders and said thickly, "Where's your home, sweetheart?"

"Where's yours", I replied. "Push off."

Then I saw him. Tommy was standing on a huge lump of fallen masonry, some distance away. He was silhouetted against a blazing building. His head moved from side to side as he tried to peer through the thick smoke. I cupped my hands and put them to my mouth, and shouted with all the power I could muster — "Tommy, Tommy, look I'm here". I doubt whether he heard my voice, but at that moment he looked in my direction, and, to my joy, I saw him coming towards me, leaping from stone to stone. I groped my way towards him, and we came together, I almost wept with relief.

In London the Blitz reached a crescendo on the night of 29 December 1940 when the fires started by an incendiary raid on the City of London were fanned by a strong westerly wind to create conditions akin to those which were later to lead to the firestorms in Hamburg (1943) and Dresden (1945).

The final phase of the Blitz began in mid-April 1941 and ended with a savage raid on London on the night of 10-11 May in which 700 tons of high explosives were dropped, starting 2200 fires and killing 1436 civilians.

Damage was heavy in the Elephant and Castle area and one of the casualties was the Reverend Christopher Veazey's church, St Mary's Newington. His wife Joan's diary tells the tale.

10 MAY 1941. A terrible night — the worst blitz we have ever had. Our town is practically burnt out. It all started when the first bombs rained down, there must have been thousands of the wretched things. One landed high up in the Church's beamed roof — which is entirely oiled wood. C. came in and asked me to

come and help him; we could see the bomb flicker and spurt, we couldn't reach it. Sixty feet high? We tried to throw heavy sticks to see if they would dislodge it — we tried bricks, nothing would go so high.

We watched helplessly, our Church gradually turning into a raging inferno. We stood inside, just a little out of the direct fire, and we watched each beam crash down as it burned through. Then, when the whole roof had gone, and we had gradually moved to the only door left for escape . . . we watched the lovely Altar catch alight; and as the flames crept up the painted wood the Saints' pictures looked as if they were people burning. We knew now that we would be the last people to worship in this huge Church. The whole building burnt with white hot flames, and as the wind changed direction, we feared that the Rectory would also catch fire — there was no water. We could hear the screams of the pigeons as they burned in the tower. The great bells fell from their moorings and crashed in a mighty rush of sparks and red hot molten metal.

In spite of being pregnant I did manage to carry 42 buckets of water from the tank of the Rectory down five floors and back for more. My feeble efforts were no use and by now my baby was jumping like a salmon going up river to spawn. . . . It was like pouring a thimbleful of water into Hell itself.

When Christopher realised that we had been beaten, he said, "We had better go off and see if someone else wants help." So very wearily we walked up towards the Elephant and Castle . . . at least to what was once the Elephant and Castle. We came to a row of houses where there were only two men and a few women trying to put out the fires. Between us we managed to get these under control, when I told one woman that I was expecting a baby. She stared at me and said "Good God!" Sometimes I wonder if my baby will survive or be born holding a stirrup pump!

On the day before the big raid, Mary Mulrey a nineteen-year-old Irish Nurse at the Kent and Sussex Hospital at Tunbridge Wells, came up to London to meet her Free French boyfriend, Pierre. After she had booked into the Alexandra Hotel they walked round Hyde Park and admired the daffodils — an odd contrast to the evidence of war all around them. As her diary reveals, the following day, all her medical skills were needed in the aftermath of the night's destruction.

11 MAY 1941. Pierre had only just left me around midnight when there was an air-raid alert. There was a momentary feeling of trepidation when I wondered whether I should go to the underground shelter, but decided that I was too tired and that it would probably be only a few bombs on the docks as usual.

I went back in to the lounge and there were long sick minutes of silence that frayed the nerves and then it happened — a whining shuddering like an Express train leaving a tunnel — the air shook with a volcanic rumbling, and a marble pillar in the centre of the room cracked like a tree trunk. In the maelstrom of dust, tumbling masonry and splintering woodwork, people were screaming. I may have screamed too — I do not know, but within seconds into the room there came a niagara stream of plaster, dust, planking and chairs. The walls seemed to burst apart raining light brackets, mirrors, clocks and chunks of ceiling. The centre of the floor where the pillar had stood burst apart and the debris thundered down to the basement. There was one terrible cry of terror from the shelterers beneath.

Suddenly I realised that I should be helping people not just standing there frozen with horror. . . .

2 a.m. Some more casualties from the Hotel were taken to St. George's Hospital and I accompanied them to offer my services. It was utter chaos, the lighting had failed and surgeons were trying to work by torchlight. I helped with the setting up of blood transfusions and at 4.30 a.m. went outside for a breath of air. The all clear had not yet sounded, but a strange hush had fallen on the scene. Across the park the guns were silent and the only sound was the muted blaze of a gas main burning in Park Lane.

I went back to the ward. It was awful — bed nudging bed and stretchers along the full length of the Nightingale type ward. The nurses and doctors looked hollow eyed with fatigue. They were still putting up blood transfusions and saline drips. I made tea for everybody.

Pierre found me at St Georges around 5 a.m. He was horrified by the damage to the Alexandra and the enormous number of casualties from the whole area.

Pierre had spent the night helping to put out fires, or trying to help put out the incendiaries.

I was dirty, covered in blood stains, and his face was

black with smoke and there was a nasty burn on the back of his left hand, but we were happy to be alive and to be together.

CHAPTER
THREE

Into Uniform

In Britain the conscription of women was introduced in December 1941. The first conscripts, aged 20-21, received their "call-up" papers in March 1942. They were given a choice between serving in the auxiliary services — the WRNS (Women's Royal Naval Service), the ATS (Auxiliary Territorial Service) and the WAAF (Women's Auxiliary Air Force) — civil defence or industry. By the summer of 1944 some 467,000 women had chosen the auxiliary services. The efficiency with which these women were absorbed, and their ability to undertake an ever-widening range of responsibilities, had a direct effect on the number of men available for service in the field.

At the beginning of the war there were only five "trades" in the ATS. When it ended, women had replaced men in no fewer than 80 trades, the majority of them skilled. In the WAAF, too, there were over 80 trades, with 95 per cent of airwomen replacing airmen on a one-for-one basis. By 1944 two-thirds of WRNS officers were replacing naval officers, notably as cypherers and in technical and secretarial work.

Secretarial, catering and domestic work were all traditional areas of employment for women, but the demands of war quickly demonstrated that they were more than capable of shouldering responsibilities which would have been unthinkable in pre-war days. In 1942 approximately 50 per cent of the new recruits in the ATS were destined to serve in mixed anti-aircraft batteries, 17 per cent became drivers, 10 per cent telephonists and teleprint operators, 9 per cent cooks, 9 per cent domestic workers of various kinds and 5 per cent clerks. A year later it was estimated that 80 per cent of Army driving was done by women — who drove, maintained and repaired everything from staff cars to three-ton trucks and gun limbers.

In the WAAF women served as flight and instrument mechanics, electricians and armourers. The highest trade group in the RAF, that of fitter, was open to them. They played a key role in the interpretation of photographs of enemy targets and in the debriefing of the aircrew who attacked them. By 1944 nearly all the Service Meteorological Officers of the Flying Training Command were women. And the weather played an often baleful part in the duties of WAAF balloon operators, who worked in conditions of great discomfort and physical danger.

In the Navy the daily progress of the Battle of the Atlantic was plotted by Wrens in the Operations Room of Western Approaches Command. Wrens manned harbour craft in all weathers, although they were not allowed to go to sea in HM ships. They served as coastal mine-spotters, a particularly hazardous task, air and radio mechanics and armourers. They trained as welders and carpenters and maintained and repaired ships in naval bases.

From gunnery training observers to parachute packers, from signallers to searchlight operators, women played a vital role in securing victory. War not only gave them opportunities denied them in peacetime but also gave them a confidence in their ability and a sense of comradeship to which they now look back with pride. As former WAAF Margaret Feldon recalls, "In a way it was like going to university. We were mostly that age and you see people change as they grow up through a war. Before the war I had never been anywhere much and I knew very little. The people I knew were confined to my local area. In the WAAF I met all sorts of people in all kinds of circumstances. I saw things I never thought I would see. And there's an instant bond between us all when we meet again today."

Young women from every conceivable background were thrown together in the melting pot of the Services. D. J. "Panda" Carter remembers her introduction to life in the ATS and her rapid acquisition of the low cunning needed for survival in the forces.

At last I had my papers to go. I had longed to join the Women's Services, but being the last one left with my widowed mother, she was doing all she could to keep me at home. I do not know how she arranged it, but a few months before she had found me a reserved post in the Admiralty in Whitehall. Each day I travelled on the Underground from Golders Green to the Strand, crushed like a sardine. The wet days were the worst when our raincoats were steaming and the smell was awful. My job was in the Drawing Office, drawing silhouettes of Japanese shipping. I longed for something more adventurous. With my call-up papers I could step through a door into the unknown. . . .

I had to report to the Telavera Race Course in Northampton for my training. It was cold and foggy when I stood on Euston Station wondering what lay ahead. The journey was cold and seemed endless. An army lorry picked up several recruits from the train. I don't imagine any of us had ridden in a lorry before, and we swayed from side to side and bumped up and down in complete silence. On arrival we were given a meal in a huge nissen hut and then taken to the huts which would be our home for the next month. We were to live twenty-four to a hut. Until now I did not know what a variety of females of my own age there were living in these Islands amongst what I thought were normal people. In my hut there were two girls from Glasgow who had to have their heads shaved because they had lice. One poor soul was in trouble every morning because she had wet the bed; but the girl who fascinated me the most was an Irish ballet dancer who screamed and shouted in the middle of the night and sometimes walked in her sleep. We were a very mixed bunch, but they would soon knock us into shape.

I was longing to be issued with a uniform, but at first it was not quite as I expected. I do not know how the sizes were worked out, but they all had to be altered. At first my skirt was nearly down to my ankles and the sleeves of my jacket twice as long as they should have been. My great-coat was as heavy as a rock, and so stiff I could not have bent if I wanted to. The most outrageous things were our pyjamas; they were blue and white striped wincyette and all the same size.

It was in Northampton on the Telavera camp that my whole outlook on life changed. I learnt that to get by one had to be very cunning. At 5.30 a.m. we started our day by lining up at the Company Office to be given work. It consisted of cleaning toilets, scrubbing floors, burning sanitary towels, lighting fires and several other menial jobs that are difficult to do in the dark on a freezing November morning. I was the lucky one — I had a torch, my most treasured possession at that time, because while the others worked I held the light for them.

Our four weeks training was like a complete new world. Each day, rain, shine or snow, when the camp was ship-shape, we spent many hours learning how to march and obey commands. I enjoyed it after a while, and even knew my left from my right. We had learnt discipline. Our uniform fitted smartly and we were medically A1, having had all the appropriate injections.

The last part of our training consisted of a variety of tests to decide for what kind of work we were most suited. It was like being back at school. We had to sit several written papers, and then take a practical test of assembling wooden puzzles, fitting pegs into holes. There were also odd bits of machinery to find out if we were mechanically minded. I had just one aim, to become a draughtswoman. When it was my turn to be interviewed by the Commanding Officer, she asked me what I would like to do. When I told her she handed me a huge book about architecture. She asked me if I understood it, and I told a deliberate lie. I said I understood it all. She obviously didn't believe me, and said I was just the right type for a clerk. I tried to protest by telling her I could not spell. Her answer was "None of us can." So that was that. My case was lost. My heart sank — how boring.

In 1942 Stephanie Batstone decided to throw in her job as an admissions clerk with the Emergency Hospital Service.

I had been seduced by a leaflet given to me by a schoolfriend who had joined the WRNS as a Wireless Telegraphist. The leaflet was about a Signal School in Lancashire called HMS *Cabbala*, where they trained Wireless Telegraphists, Coders, and Visual Signallers. As soon as I saw the photographs of girls signalling with lamps and doing semaphore and hoisting flags up masts, I knew that was what I was going to do, and nothing else.

Even the schoolfriend tried to put me off. "The signallers were out in all weathers when I was there," she said. "They were blue with cold, they got pneumonia. Why don't you do W/T and be in a nice cosy nissen hut? You know how you hated games at school."

It was true. The worst misery of my life was endured squelching about on a tilted balding field in a North East wind with someone shouting "Run girl, can't you."

I said, "I shall go there in the summer then".

Towards the end of 1942 I asked at work if I could leave a bit early one evening to go to the dentist. I went to Westminster, to the WRNS Recruitment Office. There was a poster in the window, of a healthy smiling apple-cheeked girl with dark springing hair, in Wren uniform, with flags in the background. It said, "Join the Wrens and Free a Man for the Fleet."

When I had worked up the queue, across a trestle table I surveyed a woman in a uniform jacket with buttons on the cuffs. She didn't look glowing like the girl on the poster, and neither did I. We both looked pasty. We spent all our evenings and nights down the shelter.

I said, "I want to be a visual signaller."

"Sorry," she said "I'm afraid that category is closed and there's a waiting list. I doubt if we shall recruit any more. At the moment the only categories open are Writers and Cooks. Can you do shorthand and typing?"

"No," I said.

"What a pity," she said. "Well, just fill in the form and where it says 'category' put 'cook'. I'm sure you like cooking, don't you?"

"No," I said. "I hate it."

I took the form home and where it said "category" I put "visual signaller" and where it said "second choice" I put "none" and I posted it back.

Three weeks later a buff card came with an Admiralty stamp requesting my presence for an eye test at the Naval Recruiting Office in Charing Cross Road. . . .

Like "Panda" Carter, Stephanie Batstone soon found that she was just one of a very mixed bunch. After the recruits' first lecture the girl sitting next to her asked, "What did you do before you joined up?"

"Clerk in a hospital," I said. "What did you?"

"Woolworfs, Balham High Road," she said with a grin. "Lectrical counter. I'm doing W/T. Me bruvver's a sparks. At Pompey." I didn't know where Pompey was. It sounded foreign.

The girl the other side said, "I was a teacher till yesterday."

"Where?" I asked.

"A village in Anglesey. Miss Williams will have come back today to take over. I wonder how she'll get on. She's nearly seventy." Her voice was soft and lilting. She said, "My fiancé was killed. On the *Hunter*, at Narvik. He was a teacher too. I couldn't just do nothing."

Into the melting pot we all went — conscripts, volunteers, engaged, married, widowed, single, Zara from Brasil, Rita from Balham, Cathy from Anglesey, Marianne from Barclays Bank in Aberdeen, Joy from Sainsbury's cold meat counter in Birmingham, Clodagh from milking her father's cows near Kinsale in County Cork, Maureen from being a hotel chambermaid in Dublin, with the bright lights and butter and German Embassy, Joan from helping her mother run a boarding house in Skegness, Judy straight from school, Pauline from an Estate Agents in Wood Green, Celia from the Prudential in Exeter, Vivienne, a second year nurse at Leeds General Infirmary, Patricia from a repertory company in Belfast, Betty who thought life was fun, Irene who wore glasses.

Four weeks later, out of the melting pot came the coders; sixteen weeks later the V/S[1]; and six months later the W/Ts[2]; not yet looking like the girl on the poster, but give or take a few bumps, looking roughly the same size and shape. The prototype Wren, knowing that Pompey was Portsmouth, and gash meant redundant, and slops was stores, and chokker was fedup, and rabbiting was thieving, and a bottle was a row, and a stand-easy bun was elevenses, and a gannet was greedy, and Jimmy the One was the First Lieutenant, and tiddley was for best, and to put the anchor on the bedspread the right way up or the ship would sink. We had entered the only real democracy. We weren't pretending to be equal, we were equal, and might have to go on being equal for years and years. It was a great relief.

Eventually the time arrived for kitting-up and metamorphosis into the glamorous Wren of the recruiting poster — or so they fondly hoped.

Two skirts and two jackets, a tiddley one and an everyday one; two pairs of blackouts, navy artificial silk and down to the knee; two pairs of black lisle stockings; two pairs of shoes, a raincoat, a greatcoat, a tie. Six collars, two sizes too large because they would shrink in the laundry. Six shirts, the right size because they wouldn't. Between the back stud and the front stud

[1] Visual Signallers.
[2] Wireless Telegraphists.

there was always a bulge of collar over shirt. The collars did shrink, but before they were down to shirt size they got so worn they rubbed our necks raw even when we put candle grease on. The hat, the crowning glory. A taffeta hat ribbon with HMS worked in gold on it. And, because we would work outdoors, two pairs of thick navy woollen blackouts, two pairs of bellbottoms, a seaman's jersey, and woollen gloves and socks.

We tottered back clasping our burdens, and about ten of us piled into Betty's cabin. "Look at these woollen knickers!" shrieked Joan. "Just imagine anyone thinking we would be seen dead in them!" We all packed them up and sent them to our elderly aunts, who were delighted. By about November, standing about on cliffs in the Hebrides, we would have given anything to have them back.

The skirts had the curious placket we had noticed, with large buttons. When we put them on we looked as if we had hernias. On some of us they reached the ankles and on some of us they were up to the thighs. They all had to be the correct number of inches off the ground before we were allowed out of camp. We ironed the seams to look like pleats.

The jackets had an inner pocket over the left breast. We had to keep our pay books there. With a hernia on the hip and a flattened breast on the left we had a decidedly lopsided appearance. . . .

The pièce de resistance, the bellbottoms, were our badge of office, our passport to a man's job, and in them we would swank around the camps and bases of the future with our bottoms cheekily outlined and our waists nipped in. Alas, a shattering blow awaited us.

"They're not for Wrens — they're sailors' bell-bottoms," said Maureen, shocked.

Sailors' bellbottoms were three flaps thick over the stomach, of the best thick serge. Two of the flaps were sturdily lined with ticking — one came from each side and they buttoned together down the middle. Over them a third flap lifted up and buttoned to each side seam. It was true that they were tight over the seat, but on us the flaps stuck out over our stomachs in an obscene way.

"We can't wear them like this," moaned Marianne, peering down the large gap between her waist and the top flap, as though expecting to find a baby kangaroo there.

Celia was already on her knees with safety pins in her mouth. She was the class leader — a calm, placid girl with classic features, a born mediator "We'll have to cut off the side flaps and just pray they hold together" she said decisively. "Until we go on leave, and our mothers can alter them." So like generations at Cabbala before us, we did. Without the side flaps they weren't quite so laughable, but the awful truth was that kitted up we did all look like nothing so much as Tom Kitten.

"Square bashing" was another immutable feature of the rookie's introduction to the Service. ATS recruit Dorothy Calvert recalls her first taste of the parade ground.

Before any of us could spit, they were yelling orders at us from all directions, and had us moving about like "blue-arsed flies"; the worst part of it was, not one of us had an inkling of what they were yelling about. Trying to hear each order as it was given, remembering it, and trying to get our feet and arms to work in unison was impossible, and the Instructors saying as if it was something that they rehearsed beforehand, "What a lousy shower you lot are," did not do much to fill us with confidence. The trouble was I always wanted to laugh, for the more they shouted, the funnier it struck me; I always did have a warped sense of humour. But I felt sorry for the girls who were so scared that they would faint, and have to be pushed on the side to come around again, and those too, who would stand rooted to the spot, and even wet themselves, weeping at both ends, as it were. Only then would they pack it up for a time, until the next bout, of course.

This constant drilling and marching went on and on, until I thought that the idea was for us to march into Germany, fetch old Hitler out, and then have a go at him, and believe me, nothing would have given me greater pleasure, after all the perishing square bashing we had had to do, and the blisters we had got; there were many and varied things that I alone could have thought up for him, before finally separating him from his breath. But no such luck, it was just a little of the good old British Bull that we were suffering from, at that time.

I remember one memorable day. We were on the square again, but something had happened, for lo and behold, we were all marching in step, our arms were swinging at the correct height, the hands making fists with the thumbs on the outside, not tucked in, and each command was carried out perfectly; and when we halted, our thumbs were level with the side seams in our jackets, or skirts, whichever was khaki at the time. I felt a glow of pride as our feet all thudded to a halt, as one foot, not like a badly shod caterpillar. We had done it, and what was more, Sgt. was really smiling at us, which must have meant something, unless it was wind. Now perhaps they would ease up a bit. Did they hell? What with quick march, slow march, right turn, left turn, eyes right, eyes left, right dress, and all the other things that we had to do, I began to feel like a mindless, sexless moron. Or a wind up toy.

One of the most physically demanding wartime tasks undertaken by women was the operation of balloon sites. They often lived in primitive conditions and at regular intervals were exposed to physical danger. In the spring of 1941 WAAFs had begun training to take over the flying of balloons, the role of which was to prevent low-level attacks and to keep enemy aircraft at a height where they were more vulnerable to anti-aircraft fire. Crews of 10 airmen were replaced by 16 airwomen. By the end of 1941 three RAF balloon sites a day were being handed over to WAAF personnel, who eventually manned 1,029 sites throughout Britain. Because they were not working with aircraft, they were looked upon as the "Cinderellas" of the service. One of these "Cinderellas" was Corporal Irene Storer who recalls her time at the balloon training establishment at Cardington.

A balloon in a strong and variable wind was like a thing alive. A good winch driver, though, could "feel" the change in tension on the cable, and would haul in slowly or speed up according to the "feel" of it, like a fisherman playing a large fish on the end of a line. The last 100 ft. or so of hauling in could be precarious as the balloon could sweep right down to the ground — perhaps in the next street. The winch driver needed all her skill and concentration in these circumstances.

The whole purpose of the balloons was to hold up the cables. It was the cables which were lethal to aircraft. Viewed from the ground the balloons seemed miles apart but from the air, a balloon barrage was a fearsome sight. Its aims were two fold: to prevent dive-bombing, and to keep the aircraft high enough up for the ack-ack to reach them.

Usually we moored at a "Tail-Guy" mooring from which flying again could be more quickly undertaken than if the balloon was bedded. Whoever was appointed "No. 1 Point of Attachment & Rip-line" for the day, would switch off the rip-line, shackle on wire pyramid legs, also a vertical centre leg, transfer the rip-line to the centre leg and switch on again. The winch driver then paid out again until the pyramid took the strain and the flying cable lay loose. Two girls grabbed the tail-guy and tied it to a pulley which spun round on a wire perimeter.

Sometimes it was very windy and a balloon just hauled in would be thrashing about. On one occasion during training, a girl ran to grab the tail-guy but it was snatched away again and whipped her face. In such a wind it was necessary to lay huge groundsheets out on either side of the balloon so that it could hit the deck — ringing like a giant bell — without getting damaged. It took the entire crew to shift the groundsheets about as the wind changed.

When ordered to bed the balloon, we hauled in all the flying cable and the crew took a handling guy each and threaded the six guys through blocks and on to the "Spider" which had six legs to which the guys were tied. The spider had a large pulley in the centre, around which ran the bollard cable which was attached to a bollard on the side of the winch. The winch driver changed the drive from main cable to bollard and hauled in on bollard. This pulled the spider along and the handling guys down until the belly of the balloon was only inches from the bed.

A girl had to keep the spider clear of the deck by holding it up with a short rope and walking along with it. This could be quite dangerous for her especially in the dark in inclement weather. The bollard cable and the guys were moving towards the winch whilst also moving from side to side each time the balloon yawed, crossing other stationary cables. It was more dangerous for No. 1 who was directly under the belly of the balloon waiting to take hold of the "piano" wires of which there were twelve, six from each side, shackled together where they joined the main cable. These she laid neatly down on the bed, then slung a yard — a square cushion full of straw — over all the wires and flying cable, and then — bent double — she dashed out from under the balloon, dancing over the moving ropes.

The crew then hooked on slips to grommets fixed to the balloon and tightened down the slips which were fitted to concrete blocks and sandbags. No. 1 tied the rip-line to a position on the bed. All air was pushed out of the rudder and a sack hooked over it. We then put up very high steps and, with a very long cord, a girl went up and removed all air from the fins as she started at the top to tie them up, rolling them under and tying with special knots. In very bad weather this was another tough assignment as the balloon kept bashing the steps, so several girls had to hold them whilst one girl had to hold on to the girl who was doing the tying — her hands being occupied with the tying.

Storm-bedding meant adding three extra sandbags to every slip. Snow on the balloon could be heavy enough to flatten it so as to open the valve and let out gas. So a snow-line was thrown over the balloon and from time to time this was dragged along to sweep the snow off. If it was necessary to do this whilst on guard in the night, one had to be careful not to drag the snow-line too near the stern, as if it slipped off, it would be very difficult for just two girls to get it back on again. Turning a bedded balloon into wind was a marathon, especially for two guards on their own in the dark.

Apart from maintenance, the balloons had to be hauled in in bad weather, and of course if our own aircraft were expected to be in the area. In either case speed was essential. It follows that the winch had always to be in A1 condition, and our understanding of it, internal combustion, transmission, electro-magnetism etc. had to be comprehensive. However, just in case there was ever a hitch, we had to learn manual hauling. About 18 of us, one behind the other, hauled in the balloon, to the rhythm of the counting by the male instructor. For a fraction of a second, the two girls at the front were not quite together with the rest of us and the balloon shot up again causing them to receive severe rope-burns to their hands. The girl at the front was unable to continue training for some weeks. Thank goodness I never had to put this into practice.

Stephanie Batstone became a WRNS Visual Signaller, and in the spring of 1944 was stationed at Oban in Scotland, keeping contact with ships lying at anchor outside the harbour with morse, semaphore and flag signals. Most of the traffic had been Atlantic convoys, but in the run-up to the Normandy invasion there was a big build-up of ships of all kinds.

When we were off duty, we spent more time in the YWCA than anywhere else. It stood on the green between Raasay Lodge and the town, and was a nissen hut. It was warm, bright, chintzy, well equipped, and run by someone called Miss Hindmarsh, who ought to have got a medal at the end of the war for providing all the Services in Oban with the nearest thing to home. There we sat hour after hour while the gales blew and the rain came down in buckets and outside it was black as ink and Miss Hindmarsh calmly and cheerfully fed us on hot cheese rolls and coffee. There I sat one autumn evening with Pamela, who had come off duty at 1800.

"Did all the convoy come in?" I whispered to her.

"Still stragglers," she hissed back. "I think four."

The Atlantic merchant ship convoys used the anchorage off Lismore as a gathering point before sailing south to the Clyde under escort. Usually they came stealing in and out at night, but if they had had to scatter the stragglers went on arriving at odd hours for a day or so.

Above the buzz of conversation Miss Hindmarsh shouted, "Phone for you Stephanie — it's urgent."

It was Dave. "There's a trip for you if you're off duty tonight. They want to get this convoy shifted down to the Clyde as soon as possible, and there are still three stragglers. We're sending a drifter, the *Lord Collingwood*, out to look for them and the skipper wants a signalman who can cope. You've got an hour before she sails — take all the clothes you've got, collect the berthing instructions and an Aldis[3] and Battery from Base, and for God's sake don't disgrace me and be seasick."

An hour later I was picking my way between the bollards on the pier. I had collected my seaman's jersey and two other sweaters from Raasay Lodge and an oilskin and souwester, and had been given an Aldis and Battery and three large buff envelopes at Base. We cast off and chugged out of Oban bay, past Dunollie light, and round the North coast of Kerrera towards the open sea. Behind us I could just see a glimmer of light from the signal station at Ganavan.

The skipper said, "Ye can go below lass — the lads are brewing the tea," but I couldn't waste a moment of the Hebridean night in the wheelhouse, with the little ship starting to rise to the Atlantic waves. It had been comparatively warm in the town, but as soon as we left the land behind it became piercingly cold, colder than I had ever known.

I sipped at a big steaming tin mug of tea topped up with condensed milk, and gulped down hunks of

---

[3] Signalling lamp.

crusty bread and plum jam. The skipper gestured to starboard. "We're past the south coast of Mull now — yon's Iona," he said. It was the nearest I ever got to Iona.

About an hour later the mate said "There's one!" I picked up the Aldis and made contact. I could make out a cliff ahead, slightly blacker than the black of the sea, with the familiar triangle of masthead, port and starboard light. The engine was only just audible. We crept alongside. There was a clank and a bucket on a long chain descended on the deck. I put in one of the buff envelopes. "Haul away!" shouted the skipper. "Okay bud, we'll make our own way in!" a voice shouted back.

The skipper shouted up, "There are two still missing — have you seen them?"

"The *Hiram J. Doppelganger* is about a mile back, mebbe less," the shout came back. "The *Silas X. Vanderburger* had steering trouble — she's further."

We came up with the *Hiram J. Doppelganger* in about an hour, and repeated the procedure.

It was midnight. I went below to thaw my hands. The cabin smelt fuggily of oil and wet clothes and bread and tea. There were eight double-decker wooden bunks built into the sides towards the bows. Two of the crew were sitting at the table eating. They grinned and pushed more food towards me. I couldn't bear to stay below long in case I missed anything.

In the wheelhouse, I began to realise that looking through a telescope and using an Aldis is one thing when the horizon stays steady, but quite another when it is over your head one minute and under your feet the next. It gave me a stab of guilt to remember the times I had cursed the signalmen for their erratic, unreadable signals.

At 0200 I said to the skipper. "I believe I can see her." He had a look and said, "You're right, lassie." I called her up on the swaying Aldis, bracing myself against the side of the wheelhouse, while the *Lord Collingwood* lurched and wallowed through the sea. "Yes," I told the skipper, "It's the *Silas X. Vanderburger*."

"Ask her if she can make it to the anchorage."

I did, and reported that her steering was damaged and she needed us to take her right to her berth. We crept up to the side of the third black cliff. I could see flakes of rust as we bumped against the steel plates. The deck overhung us and we moved out a little way so that the third bucket would land on deck and not overshoot into the sea. I put the third buff envelope in the bucket and put my head right back to look up and see if I could see who was pulling it up. My souwester fell off and I heard an incredulous voice say, "God Almighty, it's a girl!" Heads were visible popping up over the side. Another voice said. "Say, was that you on the lamp? Gee, you're good!" I sketched a wave and then we drew away and started to lead the ship in.

It took until 0500 to get back, up the Firth of Lorne, past the Lady's Rock lighthouse on the tip of Lismore, and over to the southern anchorage. There were enormous black shapes lying still all round us on the water. We crawled past them until we reached a gap.

"This is it", said the skipper.

Suddenly the most ear-splitting noise I had ever heard rent the air, and miles of rusty anchor chain crashed into the sea beside us. I felt as though every German between Oban and New York must have heard it. Then the night was utterly still except for the puttering of our engine as we headed back into Oban bay.

The sky was just getting light as I walked up Oban front at 0700. Time for a wash and breakfast before walking out to Ganavan to go on watch at 0800.

I thought it was a marvellous war.

Women played a vital role in Anti-Aircraft Command. Training for mixed AA batteries began in the spring of 1940 and the first German aircraft to be shot down by a mixed battery crashed in the Newcastle area on 8 December 1941.

A mixed battery contained 189 men and 229 women, including officers. At the outset there were eleven male and three female officers, the latter only with administrative and welfare duties. However, in 1943 the first female Technical Control Officers began to assume operational responsibilities on gun sites in Home Command.

On the site women manned everything except the guns. As the wartime history of AA Command observed, "They have the right delicacy of touch, the keenness and the application which is necessary to the somewhat tiresome arts of knob-twiddling which are the lot of the instrument numbers. In principle, also, women will take on all the duties of searchlight detachments. Here again experience has shown that they can be first-class on the job."

The idea of men and young women working together, sometimes in remote and physically arduous conditions, was approached with some caution by the Army. Elizabeth Lawrence-Smith, who served as a gun site radar operator, recalls: "A good many of the officers in AA Command were fatherly, schoolmasterish types, who seemed quite ancient to us, although they were probably only in their early thirties. I'm sure that this was official policy, although one or two crept in who, I'm told, eventually had 'UFM' stamped on their file — 'Unfit for Mixed'. The penalty for this was exile to a remote fort-battery halfway out in the ocean!"

The efficiency and enthusiasm of these young women, nearly all in their late teens or early twenties, occasionally produced unexpected results. Dorothy Calvert served as a radar operator on a gun site near Cheltenham.

We had been gazing at the tubes for hours, and were all feeling rather boss eyed, trying to keep our concentration fixed on our job, but it was very hard going; our eyes were trying to insist on shutting, and we were facing a losing battle. Sgt. was about to put off the inner lights so we could open the door to let in a draught of air, when on my elevation tube I saw, or thought that I saw, one "Blip" slowly moving across, and as it had been drilled into our heads, that one "Blip" without a small "Blip" behind was the enemy, well then, either I was going funny in the head, or we had got a raider. I nudged the girl next to me who checked her tube, and mine. It was there alright. We told Sgt. who of course, checked for herself. She too saw what we had seen, and rang the Command Post. They followed the Range Bearing and Elevation which we were giving them, and then they opened fire. The poor old Radar cabin was shaking with the bangs, and we girls were shivering with the excitement of it all. After a few shots the target was lost, which could only mean one thing; we had scored a hit. Sarge reported,

"Target Lost," and we were told to continue scanning. We were all very wide awake now. Oh, Boy! Our first hit, we'd show them. I don't know how we managed to contain ourselves until we were given "Stand down."

When we went for breakfast that morning, the plot of the firing was pinned on the notice board for all to see. They were all saying, "Well done girls," and "good for you," and all those sort of things, and we sat and soaked it all in, like sponges, as we were eating our well earned breakfasts. In fact our heads were getting larger by the second as we basked in the beautiful rose coloured glow.

Suddenly our Captain came into the dining hall; but what was this? He was not alone. He had with him an RAF crew, who were still in their flying gear and all looking rather mucky. We looked at each other, and then at the Captain, who was calling for a bit of hush. Then he told us that the pilot would like to talk to us. Well that was damned funny, why would an Air Force wallah want to talk to us, especially so early in the day? We all put down our cutlery and gave the pilot our full attention, especially when he said, "We have come to talk to you about your shooting last night." Well that was nice of him, but he should not have bothered, as we knew it was good, but the thought was nice. He went on to say that he would like to congratulate us too. Well I never did, we must be getting famous if the news had spread about us! Then I heard him say, "Yes, you got us, in about six shots." Well I felt as if I had been shot down. I had been on cloud nine, and I was down to earth with a bang. I looked at the others, and I could tell that they were feeling just as deflated as me. What the hell had we done? What had gone wrong? We had carried out the set procedure, so where had we buggered it up? It could not be true, nothing so awful, we had shot one of our planes down in mistake for a Jerry.

Then he said, (which I thought was super of him). "Don't take it to heart, it was not your fault, as our damned IFF[4] had broken, it could have happened to anyone." Well, he had put things right for us, we had not done anything wrong on the sets, but somehow it did nothing to make me feel any better. The thing that stopped me from howling was the fact that the aircrew were all safe. Thank GOD! That was something else I for one did not want to repeat. We took a long time to live that down, but we did not repeat it, I am glad to say.

There was a different, and more poignant, form of intimacy between the WAAFs and aircrew who served on Bomber Command stations. It was a strange kind of war for the men of Bomber Command. One night a young airman might be enjoying a pint at the local pub, the next weaving through the flak-filled skies over the Ruhr. For intelligence officer Grace Watson, stationed at RAF Kirmington with 166 Squadron, the work was both demanding and on occasion melancholy. Her duties included the detailed preparation of intelligence before a raid, attending the aircrews' briefing, interrogating them after the raid, compiling raid reports for 1 Group Headquarters and Bomber Command, the manning of the Operations Room, updating the position of decoys on maps of enemy territory "and umpteen other duties that came within the category of Int/Opts. When time permitted I would

[4] Indentification Friend or Foe signal.

accompany the Squadron Commander when he drove around to each dispersal before Take-off (T/O), to wish the crews well. It was heartbreaking when any of them failed to return. One had got to know them so well and they were all good friends. This, I found, was the hardest part of being on an operational station."

Grace Watson kept a shorthand diary while at Kirmington. An entry from July 1944, when the Normandy invasion had got bogged down and was unable to advance, vividly reveals her involvement with her work and the strain it imposed.

In the morning of the 7th we were Stood Up for two targets, one to be a Daylight, with 42 a/c[5], and the other to be a night attack with a further 12 a/c. At 0945 hours we briefed for the Daylight op, but just as briefing was over, it was indefinitely postponed. At midday it was scrubbed altogether, and we were then asked to provide every available a/c on the station, for an early raid. We were able to offer 30 a/c, a record number from this Squadron. There was much speculation as to what the target would be, and when the gen came through, it thrilled everybody: it was Caen, where our land troops are having such a tough job to dislodge the Germans. It was considered a wizard target, both from the point of view of being able to "get rid of" a large number of Jerries (we hoped), and also in assisting our own men over here to forge ahead and take the town, whilst Jerry was reeling from our blow. It put a terrific responsibility on our Bomb Aimers, of course, because our troops were only 1½ miles away, so that even a slight under-shoot would

---

[5] Aircraft.

result in our own men, and not the Germans, feeling the weight of our lethal bomb load. Johnny had been given permission to go on this trip and was as happy as a sandboy: (incidentally, what *is* a sandboy? Well, whatever it is, that's how happy Johnny was). I think his enthusiasm infected the crews when he did the briefing, for there was certainly a sense of excitement in the room.

I went out in watch T/O[6] at 1900 hours. It was a most glorious evening, with brilliant sunshine, and my feelings were once again those of pride and admiration as each beautiful Lanc[7] roared down the runway and rose into the sunlit evening sky: there was Hutch in G-Charlie; Jimmy in B-Baker; George Serrels in O-Oboe — (this was George's last trip, and we all had our fingers firmly crossed for him); there was dear Hughie in D-Dog; . . . and so on until they were all airborne.

They were due back at 2300 hours, so I went to the Mess for supper, sat and read for a bit, and then returned to the Ops Room. I went up into the Watch Office to see the first few kites land, and heard O-Oboe call up, "O-Oboe calling for the last time", and then, Great Scot, we all ducked and held our breath as Oboe roared down upon us, and just missed the roof of the Watch Offices by a few inches. This was "The Saints" shooting us up before landing. I really thought we'd all had it, but George throttled back just in time and rose up above the Watch Office, then made a great circuit, and landed beautifully. What a tremendous relief it

[6] Take-off.
[7] Lancaster bomber.

must have been to them all to feel the solid earth beneath them, and to know that their tour was safely completed.

The next to call up was my heart-warming D-Dog, so knowing that Hughie and his precious crew were back I returned to the Ops Room. By that time "The Saints" were coming in, and they were wildly enthusiastic about the whole trip. In spite of intense flak, both heavy and light, they knew that the attack had been a success. Every bomb fell in the target area, none had undershot. One after another the crews poured into the briefing room and each one added to the enthusiasm and happy excitement. Johnny had enjoyed himself and is already wondering what "his next trip" will be.

While we were still de-briefing a message was received direct from the 2nd Army in Normandy which said, "The heavy bombing attack just taken place was a wonderfully impressive show. The 2nd Army would like their appreciation and thanks to be passed to all crews. Flak appeared to be intense at the beginning of the attack but died down during the attack." This message was put on the black board in the briefing room for all crews to see as they came in for interrogation. . . .

In spite of all the happiness and enthusiasm over such a successful raid, we were all deeply saddened by the loss of S/L Weston and his crew in Q-Queenie. This was the only a/c unaccounted for, and several crews reported seeing an a/c crash in flames in the target area, so this must have been the one. I feel particularly sad because in the briefing room (before briefing began) I talked for a few minutes with "Red Mac", the Canadian Navigator, and he said, "I've got a load of candy in my room — would you like some?" I said, "Yes, please, if you can spare it." "Right", he said, "I'll see that you get some tomorrow". . . . . Poor "Red": for him there won't be a tomorrow. I don't care about the candy; I just wish that he and the rest of the crew were still here with us. Perhaps, just perhaps, they had time to bale out, but it doesn't seem very likely.

Even in the middle of war there was a place for the "woman's touch", particularly if it was applied by a WAAF officer as determined and practical as Frances Stone, who had asked to be posted to the RAF station "where amenities and conditions were worst, and I quickly found myself at an isolated unit called Babdown Farm in Gloucestershire". She quickly set about restoring morale.

During the morning after my arrival, I toured the WAAF site, and found that none of the airwomen had more than three hooks on which to hang their clothing. I turned to the Flight Sergeant and said, "I see we have to make over three hundred lockers and hanging wardrobes." She looked incredulous, and as I moved on I heard her remark to the WAAF Admin. Sergeant, "The woman's mad." Mad I may have seemed, but I was in a determined mood and this was surely the biggest challenge of all. I soon discovered that the morale of the airwomen was very low, and this must be raised. I had always found that the most important factor in an airwoman's or airman's life was to have a little locker in which personal items could be kept, and on the top of which photographs of loved ones could be placed.

I went to the Commanding Officer and expressed my views. I asked that I might be allowed to work in my office during the mornings only; all the rest of my time I wished to be on the WAAF site about a mile away. My request was readily granted. He also said I might try to persuade the Equipment Section to let me have on loan a carpenter's bench and necessary tools. Everyone stared in amazement when I got what I wanted and set up a workshop in a drying room — the only available space.

I soon found a dump of discarded ammunition boxes; the first was placed on its end, the lid screwed longways across the top, and two shelves fitted into the box. So far so good, but I explained to Flight that they must not only be of use, they must also look attractive. She went off in search of hessian, which we dyed and cut up to make a curtain for the front, to hide the shelf contents. Two more screws and a length of wire and the curtain was fitted. The first airwoman to be given one was quite obviously thrilled, and soon I had those who were off duty coming to ask me if they could help. Through their friends in the Fire Section, we had a constant supply of red paint and thinners, and from that time, as soon as the lockers were made, they had a coat of paint.

I found that, from the welfare angle, more good was being done over the carpenter's bench than in my office. Airwomen who had home or boy friend troubles would discuss their affairs much more naturally as we struggled together to undo the rusty bolts of the boxes to provide wood for the shelves. If official action was necessary to resolve their problems, they would report to my office next morning, but by then the ice had been broken and much time was saved.

Each new airwoman arrival was interviewed in my office and I remember one such case with amusement. The same evening, this girl came to hang up a pair of stockings in the drying room, while several airwomen were helping me with carpentry. She stood transfixed at the entrance before she muttered, "Ma'am, I've never seen a WAAF officer work before." She was made welcome, and became one of my most devoted helpers.

CHAPTER
FOUR

Backs to the Land

Backs to the land, we must all lend a hand
To the farms and the fields we go.
There's a lot to be done,
Though we can't fire a gun,
We can still do our bit with the hoe.

Women's Land Army song

By February 1941 Britain was an island under siege. National survival depended on the import of huge quantities of raw materials and half the country's food, but the blockade by Hitler's U-boats ensured that controls and rationing extended into every aspect of national life. The Ministry of Agriculture therefore launched a campaign to increase production of home-grown food. Between 1939 and 1941 land under cultivation rose from 12 million to 17 million acres.

In the front line of the drive to "Dig for Victory" was the Women's Land Army, an innovation of World War I which had been revived in 1939. The Land Girl, with her uniform of dungarees or stout corduroy breeches, became a familiar figure on Britain's farms;

by 1944 the WLA's numbers peaked at eighty thousand, of whom one-third came from Britain's cities.

The Land Girls' work was often back-breaking and dirty, but the women were equal to the challenge. For example, in 1941 all the ploughing on a 700-acre Gloucestershire farm was done by two Land Girls — "to perfection" according to the farmer.

Diana Hester was typical of many city girls who escaped the routines of office work for a life on the land. Brought up in Leeds, she left school at sixteen and was working in a reserved occupation as a gas board clerk when war broke out. She applied to join the WLA, but received no reply (in fact her mother, reluctant to let her daughter go, had intercepted the letter). After Dunkirk she applied again, and after much parental opposition was eventually offered her first job, on a farm in Suffolk. By the time she arrived at RAF Topcliffe in Yorkshire in November 1942, she was an experienced member of the WLA.

I stood in the crowded gangway of the bus taking me from Topcliffe railway station the mile to the aerodrome. I was jostled against a burly RAF corporal who smiled and, noting my uniform, said,

"Work at the camp?"

I nodded.

"I'm starting there today."

"So am I," he said. "I'm Joe Kildin and I'm going to be in charge of the farming there." . . .

There was only a very basic staff on the aerodrome at the time and Marjorie, Aileen and I were billetted in one of the big, gracious houses originally designed for high up officers and their families in peacetime. The rooms were spacious and, of course, we could have one each. Though furnished only with iron bedsteads, "biscuits" (three square flock or straw filled cushions to make a mattress), pillows, linen and blankets, there were built in cupboards and there was a coke boiler which supplied masses of hot water to kitchen and bathroom and for central heating.

We ate in the WAAF Mess and the food was wonderful. For breakfast there was porridge and something cooked, dried eggs scrambled, bacon, sausages etc. and huge oval slices of bread, between brown and white in colour, with butter or margarine and marmalade. There were great bowls of evaporated milk, watered down but still creamy and tasting like fresh milk, plenty of sugar and urns of tea. Helpings were generous and we could have as much bread as we liked, which was a lot because we worked up tremendous appetites out of doors.

The land girls always sat together at the top table. The WAAFs kept as far away from us as possible because they said we smelled of the farmyard, which was quite true. . . .

A farmhouse had been engulfed by the aerodrome. There was a fairly good cowshed in one corner and here two dairy shorthorn cows, Bluebell and Rosebud, had been installed to provide fresh milk for aircrew. It was Marjorie's job to look after them, milk them twice a day and take the milk down to the Officers' Mess. I and some of the others soon learned to milk so that Marjorie could have her once a month weekend break at home. Delivering the milk was always a pleasure because the officers had more exotic food than we and in the larder there were often leftover slices of delectable sweets and savouries which we guzzled without compunction.

Joe acquired some lengths of wooden fence rail and constructed pig sties in the building on the other side of the yard. He made square pens with troughs at the front. Some of the troughs we fetched from another deserted and derelict farmhouse further across the 'drome, pulling them with our bare hands out of a foot or so of slimy mud in the yard. He was a local man who had worked on farms all his life. If things we needed were not to be had on camp he knew where he could buy them reasonably in the surrounding countryside: so we soon had straw for the sties, some eight week old pigs to rear and an in-pig sow or two. We had fuel for the coppers, lots of buckets and dustbins, an old blue Ford lorry, a series of Fordson tractors and a trailer.

The pigs were fed on the waste food from the Officers', Airmen's and WAAF Messes. It consisted of potato peelings, cabbage leaves and such vegetable waste and also scrapings from plates, leftover puddings and dry bread. It was really almost as good food as the people were eating.

Back at the yard we put the waste food in coppers with water, lit the fires underneath and boiled it thoroughly for several hours. At tea time we dipped buckets of it out and carried one in each hand to the troughs and poured it in. There was a lot of fat in it and the sides of our breeches or overall trousers were stiff with grease before we had worn them more than a day or two. But again we didn't mind and, in fact, enjoyed the work.

We had a few airmen to help us, at first just Percy and later Dick, Floyd and Duncan, who were Canadians. As our herd of pigs grew we needed more land girls and were joined by Madge and May, Edna and Eileen, Joyce and Veronica (Ronnie) and Margaret.

At the same time the station was taken over by a vast influx of Canadians. We had to give up our splendid house to a group of officers and move into WAAF quarters. We had a little house in a row of four in a street of several blocks. We could go over to the Nissen hut where there were baths used by the WAAF but it was a bit smelly, not being well ventilated, and quite a distance away so we didn't go often.

Lady Celia Coates was our Welfare Officer and came to see us. She was a friend of the Group Captain and he brought her over to our billet one evening. We said how short we were of hot water and washing space and "Groupy" said we could use his bathroom and kitchen when he was out. He lived with his batman, Axel, a Swede, in a splendid big house but was usually at the Mess in the evenings.

This was an enormous boon. We always went across in twos or threes and never when Groupy was there. While one was having a glorious wallowing bath the others would be washing their clothes, including the greasy breeches, trousers and overalls, or ironing, and collecting recipes from Axel, who was a trained chef. It was all utterly innocent but some of the WAAFs got jealous and said the land girls were bathing with the

Group Captain so he reluctantly had to tell us not to go again.

The Land Girls were resented by the WAAFs because, although they worked hard, they had a less disciplined existence. Diana Hester and her colleagues also enjoyed a livelier social life.

We still ate at the Mess, smelling greasier and piggier than ever. Our billet was inspected regularly by the WAAF officers along with the others. The WAAFs had to stack their biscuits and pillow every day and fold blankets and sheets neatly on top of them and put all their clothes away in drawers out of sight. This could be done with WAAF uniform but was impossible with our big coats, macs, overalls, breeches, often hung up to dry, our gumboots, shoes and all our civilian clothes. Despite our best efforts our house always fell far short of WAAF standards and we were always censured.

And in other ways too the WAAFs were severely disciplined. Hair had to be off the collar at the back, uniform had to be worn at all times and always had to be neat and spotless, jackets buttoned, ties correctly knotted, shoes shining. And they had to be always unquestioningly obedient.

While we were such a carefree, rumbustious lot, with hair flying over our shoulders if we chose, swaggering along in our grubby, baggy slacks, merry and uninhibited, arguing with the boss and flouncing off to other jobs if we weren't satisfied. (Joe and I both had hot tempers and frequently threw pig bin crusts at each other. I could always win a fight by grabbing his thinning hair and pacify him by offering him a toffee.)

And then, having offended the WAAFs with our muck and untidiness and boisterous freedom we, being allowed to go to all the entertainments on camp, could bath and change into pretty frocks, silk stockings and dainty shoes, wave our hair, enhance our healthy outdoor faces with a bit of lipstick and powder and appear at the evening parties and shows, fragrant and charming and very feminine. We stood out amongst the soberly clad, businesslike WAAFs like flowers in the grass and the men flocked around us.

Some of the activities at Topcliffe would have upset sensitive town-dwellers.

Pig killing was something of a ritual. We got barley meal for a final fattening up of the pigs and when they were big enough we killed them on the premises, it not being necessary then to send them to a licensed abattoir.

We had to prepare a big tub of boiling water. Then Joe shot the pigs with a humane killer. This was a gun. You held the nozzle against the pig's temple and pulled a trigger. It projected a tube into the pig's brain and the pig dropped instantly. Then Joe at once cut its throat and let the blood run out of the body.

The dead pig had to be dipped in the boiling water and scraped to get rid of its bristles and then Joe gutted it and hung it up. The fat rolled into long "leaves" inside.

I loved the pigs and have always found them most

fascinating animals. But I was never squeamish about killing them. That was what they had been reared for and they had had a comfortable and well fed life. I was sorry there was so much panic stricken squealing when they realised something was going on, but pigs are very excitable and they probably were not as frightened as they sounded.

I even killed a few myself for the sake of having a go at everything, though I didn't try cutting their throats.

Miss J. White ran a farm at Inkpen, near Newbury in Berkshire. With all the able-bodied men away fighting, her labour force consisted of schoolboys, Land Girls and prisoners of war.

In January 1942, I was asked by the Civil Defence to store 5 tons of emergency food in the granary (this in case the village got cut off by enemy action) and also to be the air raid warden for the Parish. I agreed to both and almost immediately the food was delivered.

Everybody at the farm knew the food was there but we were asked not to tell anybody about it, and no one did, for at the end of the war I discovered that the village people had no idea that it had been there. It was changed about every 3 or 4 months and being beautifully packed in tins must always have been quite fresh. I was also given 2 stirrup pumps, presumably in case of fire, which were very useful for white-washing the cow sheds.

Early in 1942 orders came for me to grow 2 acres each of potatoes and sugar beet. Owing to the chalky soil and the weedy conditions the land was not really suitable for these crops but it was a wartime necessity which continued for several years, and I had to obey. When it came to harvesting the beets I needed more help and was able to get German prisoners of war from a camp near Newbury. At first they came with a British soldier as guard, but later they were just delivered in a lorry and collected again in the evening. I "ordered" them by telephone. It seemed rather like slaves. Over the years we had a lot of POWs mostly Germans, sometimes Italians (the Germans were the best) and sometimes Land Girls from the Land Army.

At the end of the war we had German Africa Corps men who had been sent back from America, and very nice people they were. I was very impressed by their "esprit de corps" and smartness, they must have been very good soldiers. I built a cattle yard with an open fronted shed with two of them, and a very good job they made of it in spite of the language difficulty, they spoke little English and my German was not very good. The prisoners were a tremendous help, I don't know what we would have done without them, and very willing workers, except one, a fair haired, blue-eyed Nazi type who became very truculent and would not do what he was told. I sent him back to camp and informed the Commandant by telephone who asked me to send a written complaint, which I did, and we did not see that one again. I did have a little trouble with them over pulling up the sugar beets. The weather was wet and cold and the difficulty was to get them to start. It is a back breaking job that has to be done by hand, and they had no gum boots (nor had we) and the ground was wet and muddy. I lined them up at one end of the field and said in what I hoped was understandable German "Now go on: START", and being German soldiers, trained to obey orders, they did, and made a very good job of it.

The farm suffered a major disturbance when the War Office commandeered part of it to be used as battle training area for the US Army. Sometimes Britain's so-called Allies must have seemed more like the enemy.

Before the war Inkpen had a flourishing rifle club and had made a shooting range on the Wansdyke, that ancient defence ditch and track which began (or ended) at the foot of Beacon Hill, along the boundary of my land. The first requisition order was for the rifle range only, so I did not worry much about it, but it was very soon extended to include about 150 acres of my land to the north of Beacon Hill. The American army made a sort of "strong point" which they were to practice capturing, north again of this, and still on my land. While the troops captured the "strong point" in the valley others stayed on Parson's hill and shot over their heads with machine gun tracer bullets, 6 inch mortars and basookers (sic). I don't know how many of their people got shot, it was a miracle they never shot any of us.

The troops would arrive in luxury coaches in the morning, leaving them to block the lane all day, walk down the hill to the battle area, (apparently American soldiers don't march) and begin the battle. Unfortunately they seldom warned me that they were coming so sometimes we were at work, ploughing, drilling, threshing, and so on in their area and had to abandon the work and beat a hasty retreat to avoid the bullets and shells, all of which was very annoying and disorganising. Sometimes they only used the rifle range which was almost as dangerous, as discipline seemed to be non-existent, the soldiers shot at anything other than the targets, throwing up empty cans and shooting at them, or at rabbits, or even people walking along the top of the Hill, and bullets go a long way. I once saw them using a flame thrower, a ghastly weapon, and they completely burnt up a little spinney with it at the foot of the hill. The consequence of all this was that the place became strewn with unexploded ammunition. They also dug slit trenches all over the fields which were a great hazard for the tractors, especially at harvest time when the corn was thick and hid these deep holes. I walked all over the fields and put long sticks in them, and thanks to the care of the tractor drivers they never fell into one of them, which would have wrecked our precious machines. Fortunately we were spared tanks which did fearful damage on some of the farms I saw.

The battles started about 10 o'clock and continued until dinner time when the ration/cook lorries drove down the hill and issued soup and rations to the troops. All we got were the empty cartons which made us envious as we were very short of protein food at that time. We did get other things, though. The soldiers sometimes left their clothing lying about, beautiful pullovers and gloves which of course we found, and kept. One day an officer came to me and said that his men were losing a lot of their clothing and did we ever pick any of it up? "Oh no" I said, but as I was wearing one of their uniform pullovers I doubt if he believed me.

There was an old field barn there with a thatched roof which was very useful to me and the troops would light fires inside it for cooking, also they would sit round the ricks smoking, all of which was, I thought, very hazardous, but remarkable as it may seem they never set anything on fire. I remonstrated once with the Officer in charge but all he said, in his American drawl, was that didn't I know that the US army had taken over the whole of the south of England and could do what they liked in it? If I had had my gun with me I think I would have shot him . . .

In July 1941 Land Girl Miss M. H. Bigwood was posted to a farm in the Welsh Border country. She has left a record of a way of life now long since vanished.

I was moved to a tenanted farm owned by the Powis Estate — no electricity, no sewage, which was common in those days on most "Border" Farms. The cantankerous Welsh farmer belittled everything I did, "What can a girl like you do on a farm?" This was his usual ploy. In spite of all this I was interested, as being a mixed farm we had everything, even to the breaking in of horses, and I had the use of a cart horse of my own. The farmer when he did work preferred the tractor for himself. In fact the two men, like myself, used horses all the time.

The only chance of a bath was to use the old butter tub, dragged upstairs filled (and emptied) with pails of water which was boiled on the kitchen fire. Again the farmer made fun of me wanting to wash.

On the weeks running up to Christmas the cider mill and press came to the farm: each farmer sending four or five horses to bring the equipment from his neighbours. I was the "lucky dog" (or unlucky) who fed the (rotten) apples into the mill, and with no such thing as rubber gloves I was usually the same colour as the murky juice which came from the press (the stain lasted for days). The pulp from the mill was spread on to sections of a thick type of sacking, folded and placed under the press. When all sections were full the press was screwed down tightly to extract the juice, which then ran down a pipe into the huge barrels in the cellar where it was mixed with buckets of water collected from the cattle trough, it was then left to ferment. Home made cider is an acquired taste and we always had a bottle with us for a "bate" (10 am break) when out working in the fields, and also a tin mug full for our drink with dinner; it was quite palatable and I never remember getting drunk on it.

We had a gang of Italian POWs and they were a very jolly and friendly crowd with no animosity towards the British. Their English was pretty poor, and their main chatter was "was I married, had I any 'bambinos'?". They proceeded to inform us of their jobs which appeared they were all Barbers or Waiters.

One day the cowman and I had to take a very lively bunch of bullocks to Montgomery Station for the train. We eventually made the 4½ miles without losing any cattle by the wayside. We also had to walk back as the farmer never even offered to come and fetch us from

114

the station. We were pretty hungry by the time we got back in the afternoon. I certainly did not envy a drover his life.

There was a Land Girl at the next farm and we became quite friendly and we used to go to the village "hops" fortnightly, in Montgomery during the Winter. We all wore evening dresses: pinned up and often with our heavy macs on, and in pouring rain cycling the 3 miles to town, and with only oil lamps to guide us there. This may seem incredible in today's world, but it was the "done thing" and to have appeared in a short dress would have been out of keeping with the times.

One winter we had a dreadful blizzard and were cut off for a month. The postman who delivered the daily paper had to carry a spade on his bike so as to dig himself out of the drifts. One Saturday I was sent into Montgomery to get the local paper and farming journals, and I had to lift my bike over several gates and fences before I got to the main road, but one never thought of this as hard work in those days.

CHAPTER
FIVE

The Secret War

INTELLIGENCE

Early in the war, British Intelligence had different departments responsible for intelligence gathering and for escape lines; later, sections were to be set up for propaganda, and for political and economic warfare. The Government Code and Cypher School (GC and CS) had been established after the First World War to decipher intercepted wireless signals from all over the world; it was here that enemy codes were broken.

In July 1940, in deadly secrecy, following directives from Churchill, a unique organization was born, called Special Operations Executive (SOE). It was divided into sections for different countries, which were then divided into a number of circuits. The exact size of SOE has never been revealed, but it is estimated that at its greatest strength in 1944 there were some 10,000 men and 3,200 women. Only half were agents, the rest essential back-up. The women agents were chosen from the ranks of the FANY and the WAAF. The FANYs had a special link with SOE, providing drivers, despatch riders, clerks and parachute packers, as well as coders or wireless operators. The latter had one essential function: to staff the base wireless stations on which most SOE working circuits depended, first in England and Egypt, later in Algeria and Italy, and later still in the Far East. The WAAFs and WRNS also had their own code and cipher staff, working on top-secret matters.

Contrary to the glamorous image portrayed by fictional accounts, the work of agents in the occupied countries was often lonely, as well as phychologically and physically taxing. The more dangerous areas of action were usually a male preserve, while women went as wireless operators or couriers, or a combination of both. Of over four hundred agents sent into France by SOE's F (French) Section thirty-nine were women, thirteen of whom never returned. Elsewhere, in Holland and Scandinavia, pockets of resistance struggled against all odds. SOE's Dutch section suffered one of the worst disasters in intelligence history: for two years the Germans controlled wireless communications and consequently agents dropped straight into enemy hands.

In a world nearing the year 2000 it is strange to think of the vital importance of tapping signals in Morse code, of crossword minds dreaming up codes, of messages passed by hand. Where now the superpowers have satellite intelligence that can convey numbers of tanks or ships, such information passed by slower methods once played its essential role in the story of victory.

Churchill, visiting Station X at Bletchley shortly after the

sinking of the *Bismarck* in 1941, said, "The work you are all doing here has been worth six battleships. It is beyond price." Before the war there had been few women at GC and CS, although two of them had been heads of section. In 1940, the number increased; they joined an extraordinary cast of scholars, academics, poets, playwrights, mathematicians and typically British eccentrics. Among the pre-war staff was Margaret Edwardes Jones. In 1932, on a visit to Germany, she had witnessed Hitler's powers of oratory, which convinced her that he was "completely mad" and that danger would follow.

In 1935, just before leaving Cambridge, I met a girl in the Government Cypher Office, and thought it might be a back door into the Foreign Office. I got an introduction to Sir Stephen Gaselee, the Librarian. He was wearing a grey pepper and salt frock coat, an Old Etonian tie as a stock, with pearl tie pin, trousers tucked into red socks and boots, looking as if he had just got off a bicycle — which indeed he had. We lunched at the Carlton Club from 1 until 4 p.m., ending with Napoleon Brandy, when he said "I can introduce you to Miss Moore . . . but I cannot say what this Other Department will think." Miss Moore invited me to a formal interview, and I got a job as temporary Abyssinian staff. My pay was £2 2s 9½d.

Head of the Government Code and Cypher School at this time was Commander Denniston. I worked for the head of Naval Section, William Clark, a chief cryptographer.

My job was to read wireless signals from all over the world. These told of foreign ships' movements, also reporting our own ships' positions, sent through to us at Naval Intelligence. I was gleaning information for the cryptographers. Already in 1938 we were working like crazy on Enigma,[1] trying to solve it by hand. I sometimes helped after hours copying figures.

In summer 1938, after the occupation of Czechoslovakia, "C", head of SIS,[2] took over Bletchley Park, a large Edwardian house near Buckingham. We moved there briefly over the Munich crisis, then permanently in autumn 1939.

During the Munich crisis everything was poised on the brink of war. We knew the German battleship *Bismarck* with eight hundred cadets on board was on a test voyage and had just put in to Vigo.[3] It was a question of where she might sail from there, as surely Hitler would not risk so many young lives? If she sailed home, it meant war; if she continued towards the South Atlantic, it was still peace. I was on duty in Naval Section over a very anxious weekend. On Monday morning, a signal came through that she had set sail for the South Atlantic: our relief was tremendous. I remember now the euphoria we felt because we had seen it from the inside. We knew we just weren't ready.

In March 1940, with the Germans about to over-run western Europe, things hotted up at Bletchley. From that August

---

[1] German military machine cipher, cracked early on by the Poles.
[2] Secret Intelligence Service.
[3] In Spain
[4] Her husband, Harold Blyth, was a wartime agent for SIS. In 1938 he went cycling in Germany — touring aerodromes with sketchpad and spy camera.

Margaret, now known as Maggie Blyth,[4] was working for Oliver, youngest brother of the writer Lytton Strachey.

The German army was moving in and getting in touch with their agents along the coastline from Spain to Norway, sending short messages, in simple book codes, in five letter groups and Plain Language (clear). We soon found they were from different countries and their importance became clear with the invasion of Norway. We moved into Hut 5 and staff arrived from Oxford and Cambridge, including the historian Hugh Trevor-Roper (later Lord Dacre), Denis Page (later Master of Jesus) and Michael Crum, the brilliant Oxford mathematician. I organised the section from March 1940 to September 1941, when I left as I was pregnant.

Ailsa Donald, from Glasgow, had been in the WAAF as a Code and Cipher Officer on stations in Lincolnshire and Yorkshire since the outbreak of war. Towards the end of 1941 came the chance she *thought* she had been waiting for.

One fine day, the message came in they wanted volunteers for the Middle East. I went into the Mess saying, isn't this marvellous, to be met with a deathly silence. Not one of them would go! . . .

I had to report to Liverpool. One was given a list of items needed and a pattern of the khaki uniform, which they gave you about £10 to have made yourself. As we were only the first or second lot to go, there were no uniforms. It had box pleats, front and back, and it was a terrible disaster. Can you imagine, in that heat, four thicknesses round your middle, what with prickly heat?

It was now February 1942, and we sailed out in the largest convoy that ever went, the build-up to El Alamein. There were about eight thousand men and forty women on the ship. But you can have too much of a good thing. One chap I met in the bar, once we had been at sea a few weeks, said "When we saw you WAAFs arriving, we thought we had never seen such a ghastly looking lot in our lives. But after a week or two at sea we wouldn't swap you for Greta Garbo!"

Eventually they reached Durban, which seemed like heaven. The lights were on and the shops were filled with goods. But Ailsa Donald, turning down a job in the RAF Shipping Office there, decided to travel on to Cairo.

We were absolutely dead by the time we reached Cairo main station, where we were back in the black-out, or rather a dim-out. I was sent to Headquarters Middle East, a place called Grey Pillars. The only good thing was you could get anything you wanted to eat, salads or fish and chips, when working through the night.

Before El Alamein, as the Germans moved towards Cairo, this terrible bombardment was getting nearer. You could hear the guns in Alex.[5] There was a notice up one day saying that it was to be evacuated, and we were to go to Khartoum. You've no idea what a panic it was.

We had to take all the files on to the flat roof and

[5] Alex was slang for Alexandria.

put them in the incinerator. There was a mass of flames with every single paper going up in smoke. The terrible thing was that the Arabs were buying things from the Jews for nothing, because the Jews were panic-stricken, running like hell to get out, selling their houses and everything. Then two or three days later the Battle of El Alamein happened, and everything was more or less back to normal.

Then we were posted to the most terrible place I had ever been and honestly even now the initials TME make my blood run cold. It was the Telecommunications Centre Middle East. It was underground, and the air-conditioning had gone to the bottom of the Atlantic. There were just tiny little air vents which were next to useless. It was hell. The Arabs would come in, sweep the floors and you were in a cloud of dust. Because of my asthma, I was gasping. I asked the WAAF Officer if I could go out while they were sweeping. She said, "It's unpleasant for everybody, and no more unpleasant for you. Get on with your work." In the end we were all fainting, so they made us go up above into the open for five minutes in every hour. They did a kind of time and motion study, like they do in factories to get the best out of you. They discovered they got more out of us by letting us go up into the air.

There were four watches, eighty WAAF cipher operators and dozens of teleprinter operators. We were sending and receiving information from all over the world, Iran, Iraq, India, Air Ministry Whitehall, Air Ministry Kingsway. You were given a machine and allocated messages, either doing Whitehall, or the

Desert, or whatever. We used to get Top Secret messages from terribly well known people. But you weren't even allowed to show them to the person at the next desk. What we used to do was say the machine wasn't working very well, so they would come and hold a bit of it and have a look.

Eventually everybody got terribly ill. We were only supposed to stay for six months, and I had been there for ten. I asked to see a WAAF officer. This woman who had never been into TME came to see me, and said "You're suffering from psychological defeat."

I said, "I'm suffering from a septic throat, Ma'am, and bronchial asthma, and I've done ten months at TME." In the end I was extremely fortunate, as I was invalided home on the *Mauritania*. It was not all bad, though, for there was a lot of fun which I would not have missed for the world. I still love, and feel part of, the RAF.

Yvonne Cormeau, codenamed Annette, was the first woman radio operator from SOE's F Section to be parachuted into France. From August 1943 until the liberation of France she was in the field, sending more than four hundred radio messages back to Britain, whilst constantly on the move between safe houses. She was radio operator to George Starr, codenamed Hilaire, one of the more successful of SOE's circuit organizers who operated Wheelwright in a wide area of south-western France, from Bordeaux down to the Spanish border. This group was engaged in sabotaging German communications (including preventing a Panzer division getting through to Normandy after D-Day, and raids on Toulouse) and helping escaped Allied airmen to cross the Pyrenees. Belgian-born, but married to an Englishman who

had been killed in an air raid in 1940, she was parachuted into France at the age of thirty-three.

Having lost everything, and liking flying, I joined the WAAF. One day in the mess, there was a paper asking any one who knew a foreign language thoroughly to put their name down. Thinking this would be for interpreting or translating, I did so, and heard nothing further for about two months, when I was called down to London.

I began my training in March 1943. The first stage was at Wanborough Manor, near Guildford, where they tried us out and decided who would be a courier, and who a radio operator, all that was then open to women. I was training with Noor Inayat Khan[6] and Yolande Beekman, to whom I was closest. We were put through our paces at various exercises — shooting straight; falling into water (a swimming pool); climbing a tree on a rope with knots and crossing over to another with two ropes, sliding horizontally; night marches; exercises in hiding.

At the end of that course we knew what we were going to do and Yolande, Noor and I were all going to be radio operators. Noor had been an RO in the WAAF already so she skimmed through the first part, only returning for the coding, decoding and ciphering and photography, whilst we carried on for a further six weeks learning the radio. There is quite a lot to learn,

[6] One of only three SOE women agents to be awarded the George Cross; the others were Odette Hallowes and Violette Szabo. She was caught and executed by the Germans.

and you have to have a supple wrist. That is why the French called it the *pianiste*. It was a very small key and everything was transmitted in Morse, the code always changing as what was used one day could not be used again.

By now it was July, and Yolande and I were sent on to Beaulieu[7] prior to going into occupied territory. It was here that people were taught "tradecraft", how to live under cover, and learned to cope with interrogations, snap police controls and searches, and other potential hazards they might encounter. The last time I ever saw Yolande was at the dentist's in London, as to my regret she did not survive the war. She met Noor again in the train to Dachau.

On 22nd August 1943 I was dropped into south-west France from a Halifax. A reception committee met me at St Antoine du Queyret, in the Gironde. It was their first drop of supplies and ammunition, and one of the dropped containers knocked off my shoe, so I landed stocking-footed! I then had to cycle to Pujols, which we reached at about 3 a.m.: ironically only to be woken very early next morning by the RAF bombing Bordeaux.

Unfortunately it was a bad time, as one of the team had turned traitor, for money, and gave away his school pals and others. He didn't dare give away Hilaire, but all the men and sons of fifteen and over were taken to Germany.

My radio set had been sent in advance so I had to wait until it was brought to me. I waited three days,

[7] One of SOE's "finishing schools".

then returned to where I first dropped and transmitted from the *chais*.[8] They had made a false bottom, which was almost unnoticeable. I had to take the machine out to transmit but kept it safely there, leaving my documents underneath. This was in vineyards north-east of Bordeaux. I used to only stay somewhere for three nights, then somewhere else for three nights, mainly in rural areas and farms but sometimes the towns as well.

Bicycles were the most important way of travelling for us, but for long distances I travelled by train. Then one needed the right papers: they had given me a card in London but I destroyed it at once. The quality of the paper was far too good compared with the recent issue of cards. So I was given a card from the mayor of a little village in the Pyrenees. "Oh yes, you're a refugee from the north." My accent was in fact northern, but I learned to speak even the local *patois*. You had to have ration cards for food and clothing, and an *Ausweis*[9] if you had a car.

When I arrived, because of the Pujols arrests Hilaire had gone into hiding in the foothills of the Pyrenees, so I went down by train and met him there. Sometimes we travelled together, but he had appalling French (though he had a lovely knowledge of swearwords which endeared him to the locals but worried me terribly) so we did not speak on those occasions, looking just like a couple who had been married for years. I did all the buying of tickets or sandwiches for

[8] Huge wine vats for the first pressings.
[9] Permit.

train travel. He went out in November 1942 and we were the only two British agents in that area until February 1944, when an instructor was sent from England for weapon training, and a courier.

My WT[10] plan started first with a sked[11] three days a week with London. Not being too often on the air allowed me time to move from one place to the other. The radio was rather heavy and was sometimes carried on ahead of me. After the war, I saw some Gestapo papers. They had found me, or rather *a* radio operator: they were quite clever, as they knew it was a woman by the touch — lighter than a man's. They looked and looked but couldn't find me because they were told it was at Castelnau in the Gers — there are eight Castelnaus!

They had DF[12] vans which were more danger in the towns, but then I used a look-out. A boy would hide on the roof with a length of thin string ending in a stone or lead, well wrapped up, which he dangled by the window. If it was anything important, he just tapped against the window with the stone, quickly hauled up the string and disappeared.

I could send messages daytime if I wanted, but that meant I had to be hidden: I did this once or twice amongst the vines. As far as possible from the house, I lay on my tummy and used the wires on which they attached the vines, before the leaves were out, as an aerial, working like this for fifteen to twenty minutes.

[10] Wireless telegraphy.
[11] Schedule, or allocated time on a certain wavelength.
[12] Direction finding.

I never did use the electric current because that was a way to find out where someone was tapping out Morse, and would cause harm when switched off. If I went off the air, it would have been marked down on a paper in London and caused anxiety. So I used six-volt car batteries — this was Hilaire's idea. They never showed us this in our initial radio training because no one had even thought of it before.

I usually decoded immediately I had received a message, because if it had something urgent I would have to get on my bike and give instructions to those concerned. It took me quite a while to code up three to five messages, which would go two or three times in a day, once in the morning or twice at night, all on the same day. Outgoing, they had to be sent and torn up immediately. Incoming, I wrote them down but only kept them long enough to decode them.

Arms were not dropped on a regular basis, but we were warned by *"messages personnels"* on the BBC when there would be a drop. Stupid wording, like *"La rose rouge est fanée."*[13] They had hundreds of them, apparently, in a drawer.

The *Milice*[14] were very active, far worse than the Gestapo. I had a lucky escape one day at the hairdressers. As often happens, I'd left my handbag on a chair while they cut my hair, then went the other side of the room to be shampooed. The *Milice* came in at that moment. The women who were sitting drying or being combed were stopped, having everything in their

---

[13] "The red rose has faded."
[14] Vichy paramilitary force, formed to combat the Resistance.

bags examined. They looked at me: not wanting to have a dribbling wet person all over them, they passed me by. In those days I was small and dark haired so I blended well with the locals.

Another close call was on a bus. I was sitting there with my briefcase, containing my papers and my cipher key, on the rack above. A German soldier asked me if he could sit next to me. I also noticed a German officer boarding, speaking to the driver. I thought things were getting a little too hot for me, so asked the soldier to let me past, explaining I was going to the "heart house" (some toilets in Germany had carved hearts on the doors instead of signs for Ladies and Gentlemen). Scratching a little corner of frosted glass windowpane, I saw the officer getting off the other end, having only been down the bus once, inspecting papers. I bought a newspaper, and came back reading it. The French driver questioned me: "Where's your ticket?" I produced it, and made excuses about buying the paper, my heart palpitating all the while.

One does, however, go beyond fear. You put it behind you, despite the constant tummy rumbles. But above all it is important to have a clear head. In that way I managed to completely lose fear, to calmly, clinically think "I'll do this, or that." You have to be quick, and not lose control.

We were warned of D-Day four days in advance, so explosive charges were placed and left hidden in position. Before D-Day our *maquis* were organised in groups of seven, called cells. We started with about fifteen hundred men. But after D-Day there were about three thousand, as around 20th or 22nd June they had come in because they foresaw that they would be paid, looked after, fed, and gain a gratuity at the end of the war.

There were regular skirmishes. At one stage, in June 1944, I was in the tiny church at Castelnau with a New Zealand airman we were sheltering when we heard an aircraft overhead: a Dornier. That worried us. Two days later, the Germans were at the top of the road entering the village, so we skidaddled down to the Auvignon river, in case they had dogs, and walked through the water to lose our scent. I was shot at then, grazing a knee and shoulder. The doctor with me took me to a farm so that I could let London know we were in trouble. He was carrying my radio set in one hand, and the medicines in the other, and I had the despatch case with the detailed papers.

After D-Day, the people of the south were longing for a southern invasion too. Finally it came, with the landing of the Allies on the Riviera on 15th August. I was still transmitting day and night. As the Germans moved out of Toulouse, then as now a powerful industrial centre, our *maquis* were the first to move in. The RAF had bombed the petrol stores, but they missed some so we finished these off.

On freeing the city, Hilaire was driving a small car, with me sitting beside him. We followed a motley convoy of lorries of our *maquis* brigade, ending up leading the whole cavalcade. The little flag on our car had been made out of parachute material. We went right into the town, while all the people were going wild. As we entered the main square, the car burst a tyre and the crowd replaced the spare wheel, lifting us up and carrying us on into the square.

RESISTANCE

Those sent into occupied Europe worked alongside the local Resistance. The best-known escape lines, helping Allied forces return to freedom and to "fight another day", are well documented. Twenty-four-year-old Andrée (Dédée) de Jongh set up the Comet Line from Brussels to the Pyrenees, making the passage herself thirty times. The work continued despite her capture and imprisonment in Ravensbrück.

For every such heroine there were others performing small tasks backstage, taking no less a risk. At the hands of the Germans the penalty was the same.

Emma Tattersall was in Paris before the war, learning French at the Sorbonne. She met and fell in love with a French-naturalized Greek scientist, Mario Nikis, whom she married in 1938.

He was doing important work for the Air Ministry. I remember Robert Watson-Watt[15] came over to see something he had invented. In 1940, just before Paris fell, Air Ministry officials told him he must evacuate everything and continue his work outside Paris. . . .

Finally we arrived at Clermont Ferrand, where the laboratories reopened. My husband was approached by the Resistance in 1942, then by the underground within the PTT[16] who wanted a reliable person to

---

[15] Leading Scottish scientist working on the development of radar.
[16] Postes, Télegraphies, Télécommunications.

make radio sets for the *maquis* in preparation for D-Day.

The PTT headquarters were in Paris. Someone had to go back and forth with messages and information. There was a Belgian, Claude, but we did not know he was a German spy. They knew everything *months* before we were arrested.

My husband usually only used me as a courier locally in Clermont, but once I was sent to Paris. I had to have false papers as I was British, although I speak French. I was to deliver my message to a man looking at a map outside the Metro station at the Place de la Concorde. Always choose a busy place.

This worked perfectly, but unhappily I had to do the same thing at Montparnasse and nobody came. There was a curfew at the time but I dared not go to anyone I knew in case I was followed and compromised them. It was early 1944, dark and cold. There were gardens on the Champs Elysées leading to the Avenue Gabriel. I sneaked into the gardens, threw myself down behind a bush and stayed till dawn, when I crawled out and took the train back.

On the morning of 15 May 1944 three Gestapo and three *Milice* came for me, having already arrested my husband in the street. His secretary, Madame Leblanc, had been arrested at the office. I had just become French but still had my British passport. We were taken to the local Gestapo HQ and made to stand against the wall until late that afternoon, with no water or food.

Madame Leblanc and I were put in one cell, just the width of a human being, with only a board to lie on.

The following night a Frenchman came for me and took me to the top floor. It had evidently been a torture room as there was blood spattered all over the place. I was interrogated: they mentioned names of friends and Resistance members, and I judged who I should or shouldn't know, and bluffed my way through. As I went down the steps, I said to the Frenchman, "How can you lower yourself to do this work?"

"I was with you and they arrested me. I am not going to be sent to Poland, I know what that means. So I chose this. Don't worry. You won't be tortured. The war is nearing the end. We are frightened, we know there will be reprisals. We will not touch a British person."

Madame Leblanc was next, and to my horror she came back with her hair and clothes all torn, face drawn, hardly able to walk. She fell into my arms, we sat on the floor and wept and she told me they knew everything. I heard my husband keeping other prisoners laughing which reassured me.

Then they took him upstairs, and he was so terribly tortured that when I saw him I could only recognize him by the coat he was wearing. The supposedly friendly guard must have had a sadistic streak because he let me see him. I would listen to pistol shots every morning and pray to God it wasn't him.

We were all taken to the military barracks in Clermont Ferrand and were there until D-Day. My husband's window was across the courtyard and we could make signs at one another. I used to sing a song because he knew my voice, to get him to the window.

We knew about D-Day that morning and the news flew like wildfire.

But unfortunately we were all taken by train a few days later to Paris. The women were separated from the men, but somehow we saw each other and he told me how sorry he was to have involved me. He told me, "You know we are going to Germany and we have another year before the war is finished."

After some weeks in French camps they were separated again and herded off to concentration camps in Germany.

We were marched out and put into a line beside these cattle trucks. We found there was a lot of white chalk on the floor. Some of the women said, "We're not going to sit on that", so they swept it away. What we didn't know was that the chalk gave out a poisonous gas causing suffocation or asphyxiation. We were forty women in a wagon. They crammed in a hundred in the men's wagons. The journey was three days, bombarded on the way. When we passed through passenger stations we would sing as loud as possible because we were still strong — songs like the "Marseillaise" and "Tipperary", which I had taught everybody. They were all French, I was the only British person. I was never frightened but at that time I wanted to die, reduced to such misery and helplessness. Somehow this was the worst time. The one thing that kept me going was the thought of seeing my husband alive again.

We arrived in Ravensbrück in July 1944, were taken

out and made to stand in the boiling heat from morning to night. It was another world, just barracks as far as you could see, very flat, and we saw thin women pulling ropes attached to a huge roller, presumably to keep the gravel flat. We were taken to washrooms, allowed to shower and all our clothes taken away. Our suitcases, filled in France with blankets and clothes, had been stolen, so we had nothing but the clothes we stood up in. Miraculously I managed to keep my toothbrush. They took my rings, including my wedding ring which I thought was a bad omen.

We were sent into a small room where we were medically examined, including every private portion of our body, to make sure we had nothing hidden. We were then given striped cotton dresses, a sort of flannel petticoat, terrible cotton drawers and plastic boots with wooden soles which fell apart. Even in July on the Baltic at four in the morning — when we were made to stand up — one had icicles on one's nose. The rumour went round our barrack "No one must be ill. Don't let them know you are ill." I later understood why.

Stupidly I mentioned that I'd hurt my back and couldn't pull a roller. The superintendent told me to go to a certain barrack the next day. No one received me, which I thought strange. Seeing a door, I looked in, and saw a dead woman lying on an operating table. She looked quite young and beautiful. I was terrified and a voice said to me, "Get out of here at once!" I never again mentioned not being able to do anything. For that was the experimental laboratory.

We were then all herded out of Ravensbrück to the

east side to Berlin where we were put to live and work in aeroplane hangars, where we riveted aircraft wings. We always had hot water, but lice were all over the place. We were woken at four in the morning and made to stand while roll call was taken. It was now winter and freezing cold, but we used to collect paper and old wrappings and put this between our clothes and skin to keep warm. If they found this, they flogged us. None of us had our periods during this time — whether from shock or malnutrition I'll never know. After roll call we were given a black liquid substitute for coffee, black bread like sawdust, and some artificial sausage. At twelve o'clock there would be a kind of soup with insects and flies, or horseradish, then again the black liquid. Absolute minimum. They didn't want us to live but they made a pretence. The wings we riveted never left the factory. I never said, "I'm going to die" or "I'll never get back." One just lived from day to day and accepted.

One day in 1945 we were all evacuated. The Russians were approaching. I was ill, so was Madame Leblanc, and we were sent in a truck to Sachsen-hausen[17] near Berlin. I often think we were sent for extermination. It was the end of April and we knew that the war must almost be over. The Gestapo were getting out quickly themselves, making a pretence of putting us on the road to the American lines. They were shooting prisoners — but only the men — by the dozens. We passed them as we went out of the gates, walking, walking, and those who couldn't keep up

[17] Concentration camp.

with the line were shot. We walked for two weeks. The Red Cross came and gave us one parcel for fifteen prisoners. We counted out coffee beans and quarters of sardines, but they were wonderful. We were put in farms, sheds, slept in ditches, anywhere we could, but always guarded. One day Madame Leblanc just looked at me, shaking her head — she couldn't go on.

Once I had no one to look after, I too gave way. I put myself with the dead, with the dying. I covered myself with my coat and thought, "They are going to shoot us now." But they didn't. Hearing marching, we thought it was the Russians — but they were military prisoners, mainly American, who had walked from Poland. We gave each other news. They gave us powdered milk. The Germans were just keeping up pretences; we saw fields and fields of them with hands high over their heads, and white flags out of their windows. They were terrified of the Russians. We never got as far as the American lines that night, but I will never forget that feeling of relief. We saw a jeep coming and they told us they were sending trucks for us. That was the end for us: we were deloused, given clean clothes and gradually I got through to Belgium.

But the worst was yet to come. When I got to Paris we were taken to the Hotel Lutetia on the Boulevard Raspail, which had been requisitioned for incoming prisoners. Our bodies were shrivelled and we could not take food. Posters were up with news of prisoners. I tried to find out what had happened to my husband. Finally this doctor came and told me the truth. They had systematically suffocated them on the way to Dachau. He died almost the day they left, 2 July. It was known as the death train — all the prisoners arrived dead.[18]

Norwegian-born Yvette Tranberg married an English naval officer, Lieutenant Giles Goodden, in 1937. On the outbreak of war she and her baby son were living in Bordeaux, where her father worked for a shipping firm. She spent several months being shunted about France as an internee, but always found ways to keep her spirits up.

I always was a terrific fatalist. In Front-Stalag 142[19] I never actually worried. The war will be over. The English are *bound* to win.

In the camp we had the most wonderful music hall evenings, as there was a lot of talent. We'd sing all the songs, and there was much humour and wit. They would tear the Germans to pieces, with the officers all sitting in the front row. But it was so clever that they never saw that it was aimed at them, and they would laugh and laugh. That sense of the absurd kept one going.

Eventually Yvette was released because of her child and found a flat in Paris. Here in due course she became a member of an escape line.

At first one had to adapt to ordinary routine living, queuing for a couple of hours to get a pound of *boudin*

[18] After the war she remarried and ran her first husband's electronics company. She was awarded the Légion d'Honneur, the Médaille Militaire and the Médaille de la Résistance. Claude, who betrayed them, was tried in Liège in 1947 and shot.
[19] Camp where six thousand Britons were interned, including the Bluebell Girls.

which was probably made with dog, then going to the market and queuing for a cabbage. The police inspected your bags, and if you had a cabbage you weren't allowed to go and queue for carrots.

Henri Blanc had the studio below us. He started by doing black market with the Germans, by selling them nuts and bolts that didn't fit. Out of this he made enough money to finance the escape route. One day my sister and I were talking in English on the stairs with another Englishman, a Jew who was on the top floor. The concierge rang through and said, "Monsieur Blanc would like you to go and have an aperitif with him." In those days it was unheard of to go and have a drink with a strange man! But we went, and he took us under his wing.

One day he came into the flat and said, "What food have you got?"

The answer was "Very little."

"All right," he said, "I'm going to send food and you're going to cook some meals and deliver them at my office." It was at the time of the Dieppe landings, 1942, and he had some Canadians hiding there.

At Christmas that year he said, "I'm bringing a Canadian Air Force chap to stay with you." My parents were coming to spend Christmas. My sister and I took him out, in the Métro, to the hairdressers, and when my parents came we dressed him up as Father Christmas!

Henri Blanc had a *passeur*[20] in Pau and took the

[20] Guide to cross the Pyrenees, *en route* for Spain, neutral Portugal and home.

Canadian down there, although sometimes he used a courier. One time as he was seeing a chap off at the station he was arrested. We were all petrified, because several of us were by now helping. But he didn't talk. He was taken to Fresnes prison, where we used to send messages to him. We used to wrap eggs up in newspaper and put pinpricks under the letters in the paper. We used to give him the news like that.

She was forbidden a radio or telephone calls, but the Germans were not very thorough and such strictures were easily circumvented.

Vera Lynn was a terrific mainstay. I used to listen to London. It was so nostalgic, one felt she *understood* somehow — that she knew how one was feeling. It did one an awful lot of good.

Others, however, were less well treated.

In the spring of 1942 I actually saw Jews being rounded up into lorries, the children in one lot and the women in another, in broad daylight. They were screaming — it was truly terrible. But before that, in 1941 I used to take Michael to the Bois de Boulogne and there were a lot of Jewish mothers playing with their small children, perfectly free like the rest of us. Then suddenly one day you saw them with yellow stars on their chests, so ashamed, trying to hide them. Then they were not allowed to go *anywhere* — use public transport, cinemas, anything.

140

And at the end of the war, in the euphoria of the Liberation of Paris, she realized that everyone had their dark side, including herself. That was what war did to people.

Then the Americans came in from the west and there was the most fantastic meeting, the Champs Elysées milling with people. There were German snipers on the roofs, trying to get the French soldiers. The crowd would say, "There, there's one there" — everybody cheered when a German fell onto the pavement. I wouldn't have thought that I could have cheered to see somebody shot, but I did. We all did.

I have another friend, the kindest, quietest person, and he assisted — he saw German soldiers being rounded up from all those awful houses where they tortured people. They were put in front of the Arc de Triomphe and machine-gunned. He stood there, watching quite happily. It turned us into beasts. But such a terrific relief to be rid of them.

Joke Folmer began working for the Dutch Resistance in 1942 at the age of nineteen. She gave shelter to Jews and students, and guided escaped French POWs towards the frontier. Nel Lind, who was ten years older, was leader of a group known as Fiat Libertas. She was arrested on 27 September 1943, when the whole organization was penetrated. Their stories overlap and intertwine, although they did not meet until they were captured. Nel begins:

I brought underground newspapers to everyone, and helped people to "dive" — go underground. In September 1942 a friendly policeman told me, "Now *you* have to dive.". . .

I was betrayed by a boy who worked for the Dutch Gestapo, and arrested. The chief Gestapo man said to me, *"Frau Süss de Witt"*,[21] *wir haben ein Jahr auf Sie gewartet."*[22] I was interrogated for weeks. I started by saying nothing, but you can't do that for ever. He already knew a lot. There were others arrested at the same time, and it is difficult in those circumstances. I said, "What will you do with me?"

They said they would keep me during the war, and I would be well treated. My name was well known in England, they told me, and they had a plan to make exchanges.

Then they sent me to the Seminarium prison at Haaren, where they kept all the people from Dutch Intelligence. Trix Terwindt[23] was the only other girl there. In my cell there was an order for officers' meals. They wanted to keep Trix alive. She asked the man in charge of the prison if she could listen to a concert one Sunday, so we got a radio.

They sent her to Germany, then two French girls came. But we kept the radio, and listened to *Music While You Work* and sang "We'll Meet Again" — we heard Vera's songs. It did a lot for the morale. But one day they took the radio away to be repaired and we never saw it again. We had heard the BBC bulletins, so we knew how the war was going.

I taught them how to do Morse code with a spoon on

---

[21] One of her *noms de guerre*.

[22] "We have been waiting for you for a year."

[23] One of only two women volunteers to be sent into enemy territory by MI9, and of only three women parachuted into Holland.

the pipes, so we could keep in touch when not in the same cell. It was always important to be with two or three; you have to look after somebody, and somebody has to look after you. Nobody can cope alone.

Joke eluded capture until April 1944; as so many of the group had been caught she tried to set up a new escape line. She had contacts all over Holland; being a girl, she was rarely bothered by the Germans. The Resistance adhered to certain procedures when dealing with shot-down airmen, so as to flush out any German "plants" and to pass the Americans off as honest Dutch citizens.

Everybody was checked back in England with questionnaires — we sent their names and dogtag numbers over by wireless. Then in Holland some police stations worked with us, telling us from the German telex whenever and wherever a plane was shot down, and how many. We had to make sure to give the airmen names without "R" or "G" in them, as they pronounced them wrong, and to make sure they slept in the trains so they didn't talk.

After my capture, when they questioned me in Scheveningen they said, "Why don't you confess you have helped these five pilots in '43?"

"Well," I thought, "if that is all . . ." They knew nothing of over a hundred afterwards.

The trial of thirty-five Dutch and Belgian members of Fiat Libertas took place in July 1944, after D-Day. Both Nel Lind and Joke Folmer were condemned to death. Joke, who had been kept in the concentration camp at Vucht, takes over the story:

We were waiting to be executed. They even sent us a priest. But then Arnhem happened, so instead we were put on a train for Germany, without papers (our death sentences). The papers travelled behind us, missing us at each place by a day or a week: a history professor sent them to us after the war.

German prisons did not want to keep us, as we had no papers. So we were ten days here, eight weeks there, constantly on the move from prison to prison — east, west, north, south. Many times it was in winter without food or drink.

Keeping as clean as possible even in these circumstances was one way of maintaining morale. There were other psychological boosts, too.

I had a handkerchief of my father's. I kept a needle hidden under my skin (like a blister, one feels nothing). We pulled threads out of everything, even found some on the barbed wire. We exchanged different-coloured threads and made each other presents. I took that handkerchief everywhere with me, and to stop them finding it I always had it in my hand, sniffing it. They wouldn't want something infected with bacteria!

Once I was six weeks in solitary but I had my paper clip, which is the most beautiful thing. You can scratch a calendar on the wall, you can make figures out of it, you can write poems . . . with a paper clip everything is all right.

Finally, while they were being kept for a period at Waldheim

prison near Dresden, they were released from their ordeal. But their change of fortune was two-edged — their liberators were notorious for their treatment of women. For once, as Joke recalls, the Dutch women rejoiced at the starvation diet that had been imposed on them.

We thought to be liberated by a nice Swedish Red Cross man with chocolates, but it was drunken Russian soldiers. They didn't open the men's prison — just the women's. But because we were so thin, they took the well-rounded German helpers and left us. We opened the men's prison, as we knew there were some Dutch there, with the keys that had been left. There was no one in the guardhouse. Then we walked, having found a map showing the Elbe was four days' walk.

Nel takes up the story:

Because I now weighed only 35kg,[24] we went rather slowly. At Riesa we got a rowing boat; we painted the name *Montgomery* proudly on it. Then we got a pass from the Russians, which we could not read. We learned afterwards that it said, "These fools try to get on by boat. Let them through." The bridges were all blown and passing was often very difficult.

A few days later the Russians shot at them, took their boat away and carted them off to a camp full of thousands of disorientated ex-prisoners. Joke described what happened next.

[24] 5½ stone.

The Americans had a camp with Russian prisoners and wanted to do a straight swap. The Russians marched one way, we went the other.

Nel had an infected leg, so they stole a cart in which to wheel her to freedom. Through generally outwitting bureaucracy, in June 1945 they managed to fly home in a bomber. Its name was *Last Chance*.[25] But there were other aspects of Resistance work apart from helping those in hiding. Intelligence gathering networks abounded. It was important to establish ways of communicating with their own people, via newspapers, and also to relay information to the Allies.

Jos Gemmeke had been something of a tomboy as a girl. By the age of seventeen she had gained a nursing diploma, and then war broke out. Friendship with a student in the underground press led to a Resistance career under the codename of Els van Dalen. She survived the war almost without a scratch, braving numerous adventures.

At one stage SOE dropped a wireless operator but the transmitter was stolen on arrival. Another agent had a transmitter but no crystals. By matching the two together, they carried on an intensive exchange of messages with England.

You often stayed up at night to receive messages. I was coding and decoding the telegrams. If they had listened to us more in London probably not so many people

[25] Joke Folmer holds the George Medal (Civil) from Britain; the US Medal of Freedom (and palm); the French Croix de la Résistance; the Dutch Resistance Cross; and the Dutch Military Medal, the Bronze Lion, which Nel Lind also holds. The discrepancy between the number of their decorations is only, as Joke generously points out, because Nel had the misfortune to be caught too soon. They are both active members of the RAF Escaping Society, which supports the families of those who ran the wartime escape lines.

would have died in the slaughter of Arnhem. But they didn't trust us because of the *Englandspiel*.[26]

Once I went with a broken wireless set in a basket full of flowers, knitting and things, to deliver it to be repaired. I always went by train. As we neared Vucht I saw the Germans coming along my carriage, making searches. Luckily on the platform I saw the boy who was coming to fetch it. The SD[27] stopped me.

I said, "One moment, please", and opened the window, handing the boy the whole basket and saying, "Give my love to your mother." Then I closed the window.

The German said "Where is your luggage?"

I had no other luggage. It never occurred to him to think what I might have handed out of the train.

After Arnhem, in October 1944, there had to be someone who went to Prince Bernhard[28] with the latest news of the firing sites of the V1 and V2 rockets. I thought it best a girl went. So I went by bike, with all the microfilms containing the information in my coat shoulderpads and also behind the mirror of my powder compact. To travel, you had to have a permit. I obtained papers from a famous pyschiatrist, Dr Hoelen, who taught me to feign a nervous "tic" so that I became a "nerve patient", badly needing to return to my parents in the south. The German Regional Commander of The Hague, Zimmerman, was also his patient and had to sign the papers. I will never forget

---

[26] Deception by German counter-intelligence resulting in capture of agents and equipment.
[27] Sicherheitsdienst — security police.
[28] Queen Wilhelmina's son-in-law. The royal family were in exile.

going to his office: a very big room and everywhere there were *CATS*! I hate cats, but it was very good as I only looked at the cats and not at him.

My bicycle had a wooden front tyre and a rubber back tyre. It was difficult to cross the rivers because the English were moving in, the Germans moving out, and few Dutchmen were allowed to pass.

British planes were swooping down, firing at the Germans on the dyke. Aircraft were strafing the bridge at Heusden, which I needed to cross. As the Germans were hiding, I took my bike and went quickly over. It was an inferno. I got shrapnel in my wooden tyre so I had to walk the rest of the way to Vucht, where I had a safe address. That night Vucht was liberated.

Next day I travelled to Eindhoven, where the chief of intelligence asked me to hand over the information. I said, "Under no circumstances", because my specific orders were to hand over to Prince Bernhard personally, which I did the next evening in Brussels.

Soon afterwards she was sent to England, to be liaison officer between SOE and the Dutch Intelligence Service. Wanting to return to Holland, she asked to do a parachute training course.

Only three women were parachuted into Holland. One was taken,[29] the second broke her legs. In March 1945 I parachuted on a terrible night. They threw me out too low from a Stirling, and I hurt my back. It has given me trouble ever since.

[29] Trix Terwindt.

She had been given an assignment for SOE and the American OSS, which was cancelled as the war neared its end. She was transmitting up until the Liberation. Her postscript is sobering:

When I was in London and the V2s came, everybody went down below. I never went down, because that was an open fear. In Holland it was a different kind of fear, because you were never *free*. Years afterwards, when a car stopped and I was asleep or a car door closed, I was next to my bed ready to take flight. You never had one moment of peace, you were always on your guard. I still hate it in a restaurant, being in the middle of the room. I always go and sit in the corner so I can see everything. I hope nobody will ever have to go through that again.[30]

Belgium had been occupied since 1940. Both the women whose stories follow helped with intelligence, and both by extraordinary chance were on the *"Train Fantôme"*, with its cargo of fifteen hundred prisoners destined for the German camps, that was saved by the Allied Liberation of Brussels in September 1944.

Françoise Labouverie worked as a guide and courier, knowing that all the time one false move meant capture and all its consequences. She worked within France before returning to Belgium and working closely with Colonel Pierre Haumann, codenamed Etienne, who ran the Tégal network. Inventing as cover a "Madame Jourdain", to whom she was secretary from Tuesday to Friday, enabled her to run the Brussels office.

[30] Jos Mulder-Gemmeke is the only woman holder of the highest Dutch honour, the Militaire Willems Orde. It is the equivalent of the Victoria Cross, awarded for exceptional courage.

Etienne first tested her with a mission to Carcassonne in France. In due course she joined up with him again: he was now in Brussels. Apparently she had passed the test, for he recruited her as a full member of the Resistance.

He simply said, "Will you work for me?"

I answered without hesitation, "I will."

It was as simple as that, as solemn for me as a promise of marriage — as irrevocable a promise and as happily given.

Now began the task of inventing "Madame Jourdain" as part of her cover. The fictitious employer's flat would become the Brussels headquarters of the group. Etienne had set up the *réseau* — network — with his French wife, Paulette.

His first task had been to choose a "pen name" for himself and his *Réseau*. When he was asked to make his choice, he gruffly answered *"Ça m'est égal!"* ("Whatever you like!") The others laughed, I imagine, but Tégal he remained. His work had grown quite successfully in spite of heavy setbacks and he now had a number of agents covering the whole of Belgium and collecting information. The movement of troops, reports on factory production, results of RAF raids, celebrities passing through Belgium, changes in uniforms, suspicious activities, even rumours, had to be reported as of course *"il n'y a pas de fumée sans feu."*[31] As there were many services like ours, all presumably sending the same information, we hoped Whitehall could sieve it all and separate it

---

[31] "No smoke without fire."

150

into facts, well-founded rumours and just plain invention.

For those first few weeks, I had to content myself with typing out the information they supplied me with, and reproducing sketches so that they could be photographed. At night we had long sessions with Etienne's beautiful camera, producing the microscopic films a courier would take to London via France and the Pyrenees.

But soon I was sent out to gather the information myself, and I met many of the wonderful people who were helping us at the risk of their lives. People without names, just a number, or perhaps a nickname; people who, without fuss, without heroics, would produce regularly information we wanted about their village, their factory, the petrol pump they served.

They came and they went, leaving no trace, leaving no addresses, so that we couldn't contact them at all unless we had pre-arranged dates, and one date missed might mean weeks of silence until, somehow, contact could be renewed.

Compared to the risks taken daily by the members of an escape line, the life of an information agent was almost as regular as that of a businessman visiting his representative in the country, entertaining potential customers, or working in his office. But it was a routine life sharpened by perpetual dangers, peppered with adventures both tragic and comical, a life of constant alertness, when the slightest relaxation might cost lives.

One day, as she was cycling towards the flat where her

colleagues were waiting for her, she realized that nemesis might be near.

A black Citroen was parked in front of the next block of flats, and the concierge had come out of his lodge to talk with its four occupants. I did not need to look at the number plate (415 519 — all the 415 series were Gestapo cars) to be absolutely sure of the identity of the visitors. I could not go away and warn the others by telephone, they had seen me coming, and if I was their prey they would follow me. I had to go in.

I got off my bike and pushed it into the hall, hoping they wouldn't notice it trembling in my hands.

I climbed up to the second floor and drew Etienne to one side.

"Have you seen the car outside?"

"No — Oh God, the Gestapo! Who is the bloke talking to them?"

"The porter of 74."

"Do you know him?"

"No, but he is always standing on the doorstep. He must have seen me coming in and out many times. And you."

The others had joined us and Etienne took command.

"The worst thing we can do is to panic and run away."

"We could leave one at a time," suggested Bob.

"So that they have a chance of following each of us separately? No. In any case, we've got work to do before we can leave the place. First let us wait and see what they do. If in half-an-hour they are still watching, we'll have to start destroying evidence."

Our four friends had not left their car, the concierge was still talking to them. After twenty minutes of this, a hoarse whisper came from Franz, who was watching.

"They are going! They've gone."

We watched the black Citroen disappearing. "False alarm!" said Etienne, "Now to work boys . . . and girls!"

I went to the kitchen to put the kettle on and as I came back into the dining-room, I glanced over the heads of the others, at the empty space behind them, the building site for sale, the waste ground full of rubbish, the solitary house on the square, and beyond it — one car!

"Etienne, they haven't gone away, they are watching us from over there!"

There was complete silence while we all watched. Etienne was the first to break it with his usual brusqueness.

"Don't stand there gaping like a lot of silly children. We have got work to do. All of us empty our pockets into the fire, where are the matches?"

"Here — but Etienne, there's ten-tenths blue sky, they are sure to see we are making a fire, and to guess why."

"Yes, that's why we have got to hurry. The more we can burn before they come, the less evidence they'll find."

The flat had been used as an office for nearly six months and Etienne had brought me for safe keeping many of his own files, and though we were very careful not to keep any unnecessary papers, there was an incredible amount of files and documents in my wardrobe, in the kitchen cupboard, all over the place.

The little stove was stuffed to overflowing. In our anxiety to see the job done, we overdid it, and more than once we had to relight the fire. The sky must have been black with smoke. I could imagine it as an enormous black cloud billowing out of my little chimney pot up there on the roof, enlivened by millions of sparks.

The Gestapo never gave up the watch for one minute, but they had come a little closer.

Although we had to destroy all we could, Etienne insisted on some documents being kept. Their importance to London was worth all of our lives.

In the full glare of the Gestapo car's headlights, the *réseau* said farewell. To give themselves the best chance they went in different directions, each of the five men carrying an empty decoy suitcase. With every second they expected shouts, shots and arrest. . . .

Nothing happened, nothing whatever. Soon I could hear only my own footsteps echoing in the empty street. Then a car started and gently made its way home. Was it possible they hadn't followed any one of us? That they had let all of us escape after such a damaging evening? What a catch they had missed. Two Réseau-leaders, a complete Réseau including a radio. Were they complete fools? or so disciplined that they had followed to the letter their instructions to keep a watch on me and never to interfere?

Well, I was free, and I had the precious papers, but where would I go with them? It was past curfew time, not a tram or a bus to be found, not a soul anywhere.

Eventually she found safety and a bed for the night. But later they were all captured and Françoise was put in prison.[32]

Also on the "*Train Fantôme*" was Marie Eugénie Jadoul, a fellow Belgian. Under the codename of Minouchat she worked for network Zero, an intelligence and escaping organization linked with MI6.

I had a small house in the village of Gottechain, from which I went to work as an agricultural worker on the airfield of Beauvechain. Of course at the same time I was noting what was going on, passing the information each week, how many aeroplanes etc. This was micro-photographed and sent to England. One day, I noted that they had put dummy wooden aeroplanes on the runways. Five days later, the RAF let them know they knew their game, by dropping wooden bombs . . .!

There were many other amusing incidents in Minouchat's war.

One day at Gottechain an aeroplane passed over the house in flames. My colleague René Ponty and I retrieved the pilot, who was very groggy after a knock on the head. Walking back we heard German cars, and had to throw him in the ditch and ourselves on top of him. They did not see us, but when we got to the small

[32] Françoise, Etienne and all their *Réseau* were on the "*Train Fantôme*" and so survived. She was awarded the Belgian Croix de Guerre. After the war she devoted herself to working with refugees — for which, ironically, she was awarded the Verdienstkreuz by the Germans.

farmhouse Germans came shouting, *"Engländer hier, Engländer hier!"* I thought fast. We had no fertiliser during the war, but there was a pile of white phosphate powder in the distance, making a kind of white mound. I pointed this out and they went racing off, thinking it was a parachute. This gave us time to hide Bill in the attic. . . .

Later the Germans came again to the village, looking for airmen. All the peasants, because of the food shortages, had hidden animals. In the corner of one house the soldiers saw a large shape with a white cloth over it, and automatically fired at it with their machine guns: another pig being salted in the process of becoming ham! The sheet was only to keep the flies away.

It was finally fifty-eight rabbits that saved Bill. We had left for Brussels, leaving him to sleep for two days, and the Germans came to the village. A farmer's wife was in her garden when they blew their whistles and raced into her small stable. "There's something hidden here. Come quickly." They climbed a ladder and broke the roof. At that moment, one rabbit did a major performance of drumming with his paws. They saw him, and fortunately collapsed laughing. They abandoned their search.

Not every marriage shared the agonies of war in the same way that Emma Tattersall's did. For Minouchat the situation was different and potentially dangerous.

My husband was pro-German and in any case we were living apart. He had not the slightest idea of my activities but I was very wary of him. He thought I must have a lover, and had me followed.

We had some of our people working inside the Oberfeldkommandantur in Brussels: some of the tarts that the officers liked. They arrived early, and left when the offices opened, reappearing again when they closed. There was an important plan on the wall. One of our ladies succeeded in removing it. Six or seven of us were at Ponty's house where we worked all night to copy this plan. At 11 p.m., with the curfew, everyone should have gone home, but we worked through.

The next morning at 6 a.m. *dring dring* at the door. We froze. The Gestapo. All the plans were on the table. One thing to do, go down to the cellars, which were linked to the sewer network underground. As we did so, *dring dring* again. The Gestapo don't ring twice.

Cautiously Ponty looked through the spyhole. "You'll never guess who's there! Your idiot husband with the police!" So we rushed everything to the cellar and Ponty went to his workshop, quickly blacking up to make it look as if he had been working. He didn't open the door. At 7 a.m. some workmen arrived and the detectives told him, "We're here to get your boss *in flagrante*", came into the house but found no one except an oil-covered Ponty, fresh from mending a machine. Later on the police commissioner gave me a copy of the report saying that it was most certainly a bachelor's home — because the washing-up hadn't been done for days!

In July 1944 Minouchat was arrested after the head of Zero had been captured; in his pocket was a paper incriminating

her. She was taken to St Gilles prison and interrogated by the
Geheime Feldpolizei.

They had two levels of questioning. One is brutal and
intimidating. The other, playing on all weakness, more
psychological. I am not very religious, but I saw a
church spire out of the window, and believe me, I
prayed that day.

Imagine three hundred cells with up to seven people
in a cell. We heard the news of the Liberation of Paris
and began banging with anything we could find *boom-
boom-ber-boom.*[33] The Germans ran in all directions,
thinking it was a revolution.

They took us in trucks to the Gare du Midi. We
were obviously bound for Germany.

**This was later known as the *"Train Fantôme"*, and with the
Allies so close the engine crews and Resistance did
everything in their power to prevent it reaching Germany.**

The driver ripped the brake from the first engine. The
second driver feigned an accident and had to go home
sick. The third driver arrived with three SS men on the
engine beside him: this time they were taking no
chances. The station was a cul-de-sac, and he said he
could not go all the way to Germany backwards: he
needed to turn the engine. So he turned the train at
Hal, but then set off for France instead of Germany.
We were fifteen hundred people on board — all those
from the Brussels, Paris and Lille prisons who had

[33] The opening bars of Beethoven's 5th Symphony, used as a
rallying cry in occupied Europe.

been condemned to death. We were about a hundred in each cattle truck. We took the direction of Malines, where the engine ran out of water for steam. The Brussels station chief had phoned to ask them to sabotage their water pump.

The Germans filled up the water tank with buckets and the Gestapo gave the order to go via Liège to Aachen. The driver shot across the correct turning and brought the train to a halt at the Gare de la Petite Ile, just outside Brussels. It had taken thirty-five minutes to return, instead of twenty-four hours to leave! Here there were trains of wounded German soldiers, troop trains — the retreat. Various ambassadors and the Red Cross tried to negotiate with the Gestapo, who still maintained we should all be shot.

At that moment the Palais de Justice began to burn — not because the Resistance had set fire to it but because the Germans in their panic were burning all their records. Negotiations broke down with the threat of the Allies' arrival. The Germans opened the wagons and we ran free. The station was near the abattoirs. The good people had already liberated the cold chambers, and I found myself running into what seemed like an army of pigs: each man was carrying half a pig!

At four o'clock that afternoon, Allied tanks rolled in and Brussels was finally liberated.

CHAPTER
SIX

Prisoners of Japan

At 6.45 a.m. on 7 December 1941 Japan entered the war, launching a devastating surprise attack on the great American naval base at Pearl Harbor on the Hawaiian island of Oahu. Neither the Americans nor the colonial powers in the Pacific, the British and the Dutch, were in any way militarily prepared to stem the tide of Japanese conquest which followed. For six months the Japanese ran riot, carving out a huge Pacific empire which put even Hitler's victories in Europe to shame. By April 1942 the islands of Guam and Wake, the Philippines, French Indo-China, Burma, Thailand, Malaya and the Dutch East Indies, three-quarters of New Guinea and Papua, the Bismarck Archipelago and a substantial part of the Gilbert and Solomon islands were in Japanese hands. To the north they threatened the Aleutians and the approaches to Alaska; in the west they were encamped on the borders of India; to the south they menaced Australia.

The British colony of Hong Kong had surrendered on 25 December 1941. Malaya, with its rich resources of rubber and tin, was over-run in fifty-eight days. The

Japanese then mounted an attack on Singapore where British resistance came to an end on 15 February 1942 and some 130,000 troops were taken prisoner. The pre-war colonial powers never recovered from these shattering blows.

Swept into internment were thousands of European women and children; they were eventually housed in prisons and camps where the conditions were never less than capriciously brutal and sometimes a great deal worse. For those refugees who fled Singapore, crammed like cattle in a small armada of ships, nemesis frequently lay waiting in the narrow Banka Straits where the ships were sunk at will by Japanese aircraft and warships. Like so much flotsam, the survivors were washed up on the beaches of Banka Island. The next stop was the camp at Muntok on the Sumatran mainland, a place which was to become particularly dreaded and has been described as a "gateway to hell".

The Japanese, who had nothing but contempt for the defeated colonialists, inflicted endless humiliations on their prisoners and, as the end of the war drew near, subjected them to near-starvation and the threat of mass slaughter. Attempts by the women to assert their individuality were greeted with incomprehension and rage. At all times the behaviour of their captors was unpredictable, veering between sudden, self-interested acts of apparent humanity and seemingly irrational surges of aggression.

Some women, accustomed to the luxuries of expatriate life and previously secure in their status on the colonial ladder, were utterly broken by the experience. Their world had been turned upside down and they could not come to terms with it. Others remained defiant. Cut off from their menfolk, constantly menaced by exhaustion and disease, they nevertheless picked up the threads of normality amid scenes of suffering and despair. They found comradeship as women, laughter and even beauty in conditions of the greatest hardship.

Mrs M. M. Reilly, who had been working as a Cypher Officer at Government House in Singapore since March 1939, has left a sardonic picture of the unblinking complacency with which the colonial administration treated the threat of war with Japan.

A conversation took place between the Governor of Singapore, Sir Shenton Thomas, and myself on Saturday, 6th December 1941.

He came into my room and sat down on the edge of my table and very solemnly said "Well, Mrs Reilly, I have got bad news for you. We are at war!"

I put down my pencil and said "Well we've been expecting it for a long time now — let's be thankful it didn't happen a year ago when we had that scare."

He looked at me over the top of his glasses and replied "Oh! but you didn't ask me with whom we were at war."

I answered "But of course, you mean Japan."

At which he laughed and said "Ha! I thought I would catch you — No, we are at war with Finland."

As he walked away laughing, I called after him "Oh! I thought you were going to prepare me to expect a Jap bomb on my head any moment."

At that he returned and said "What did you say! Japanese bombs in Singapore! You can take it from me there will never be a Japanese bomb dropped in Singapore — there will never be a Japanese set foot in Malaya."

On Monday morning about 4 a.m. 8th December, the Japs bombed Singapore!

On 9 February Mrs Catherine de Moubray, the wife of a British businessman, began work as a VAD nurse at Singapore's General Hospital. The place was rapidly becoming a shambles and the chances of evacuation were slipping away.

13 FEBRUARY 1942. First really shattering day. Middle of the morning news that all women were to be out of the Gen. Hospital by 3 p.m. Eventually by midday discovered it was *not* an order, merely allowing anyone who wanted to go, to go. Meantime with blitz on so incessantly the place was a shambles, entrance hall literally running with blood, ambulances arriving every minute. I moved to work permanently in Ward 4 — and eventually forty-two sisters and a good few VADs stayed. All afternoon we kept admitting more cases, on the verandah, onto lounges, onto mattresses on the floor, Chinese, Tamils and a child or two mixed up with military casualties.

They were shelling again in the afternoon, probably looking for guns situated much too close to the hospital, and the first two shells hit. One the roof of one theatre, the other the top of the roof of the sisters' quarters — no casualties thank god. I went off duty to collect my baraog[1] and bring it over to G's room as I intend sleeping there. Thank God the bombing lets off at dark, and even the shelling doesn't seem so frequent.

I put a mattress on the floor of G's room, but I was hardly off duty, as the little bombardier Sadd in the same room, shot probably through the lung, was restless, and G got two lots of dope, and then had nightmares which led him to try to get out of bed, and I was up roughly every half hour.

14 FEBRUARY 1942. Bombing and shelling continued all day, and the rush increased: into the bargain the water failed (or was it last night?) We were assured it was merely a break in the main, due to bombing, and there *was* water on the lower levels — so it was carted to the hospital and we all filled buckets and big demijohns and carried them up to the wards. Fletcher and I spent our time pushing lighter wounded out onto the verandah or in the centre corridor where most of them spent their day in any case on account of the bombing and shelling — beds endlessly being shifted — feeding getting more and more difficult, with more Asiatics being admitted, and the washing up question with water so scarce. The place became filthier and filthier.

On 12 February Miss Shelagh Brown and her mother embarked on the *Vyner Brooke*, which had been commandeered by the Navy as part of a makeshift evacuation flotilla. The *Vyner Brooke*'s destination was Batavia in Java, but as Shelagh Brown's diary records, the voyage ended in the Banka Straits.

[1] Bedding.

14 FEBRUARY 1942. Breakfast at 10 a.m. a mouthful of hash and ship's biscuit. Looking forward to Batavia, a bath and a good meal. Olga Neubronner is a little better — she was in a cabin, being pregnant. About 11 a.m. plane sighted. Burst of machine gun fire. Ship moves on. 1.00 p.m. Tea issued with little milk and sugar. Syren goes. Ordered to take cover in saloon. Six bombers. Four attacks. Three near misses and thrown off ground. Fourth, a direct hit on boilers. Terrible smoke and wreckage. Go on deck. Fire on deck where we had been sitting that morning. Get near boats. Planes return. Machine gun us. Boats already wrecked. Ship listing. One boat lowered. Told to go down rope ladder. Mummy descends. I luckily fall. (Forgot also to hold onto life belt but neck did not get broken.) (Mrs Macleod goes down rope and takes the skin off her hands.) Swim away from ship — and the kindly English sailor sees me and tells me my Mother is searching for me. So I swim back towards her and find that her boat had capsized, being damaged and she is hanging onto a mast with a Chinese boy and Olga Springer. Malay boy joins us & 3 Australian nurses. Have stretcher to hold onto too. Olga Springer very bad and drowning. Keep away from ship — ship rolls over — all in about under ½ hour. Hot oil — see raft. Have to pass through patch of oil and a sister produces some clean cotton wool from under the sea so that we can wipe our eyes! Join raft with a badly burnt sailor on it. Settle down to a dismal cold and terrible night holding onto raft.

15 FEBRUARY 1942. Dawn. About 2 miles from coast.

Small Japanese barges continually passing carrying troops to shore. Shout and they take no notice. Reach a Malay fishing boat and 3 get in and try to tow raft. Very difficult and make little progress. A returning barge hears our shouts and turns to pick us up. Can hardly stand and so sit over hot engine pipe. Japs cut open coconut and give us water from coconut — mouths too swollen and sore to drink. Take us to shore. Lie down on sand. Many Japs crowd round and stare. One speaks Malay (as the Malay RNVR boy does not want them to know he can speak English Mother is the only one who can converse and translates for the Australians). Some give us raisins, pepermints and a bottle of soda water. Air Raid. Lie down under coconut tree. Soon Japs give us a plate of rice, tinned food, rambutans, tin of milk. Mouths too sore to eat, and flies on wounds etc. Rest and dry in sun. Terrific heat. About 2.30 p.m. show us to a filthy Indian or Malay hut. Too exhausted to care much about dirt. Lie on earthy floor. Place full of sacks of floury stuff. Hen sits on a sack and lays an egg! Gift of God.

Shelagh Brown and her mother joined several hundred shipwrecked survivors in Muntok, Banka Island, from where they were transferred to camps in Palembang on the Sumatran mainland after two weeks.

Phyllis Briggs was a nurse who had spent her last few days in Singapore working in a maternity hospital which housed air raid victims. On 13 February she boarded the cargo boat *Mata Hari* on a voyage as doomed as that of the *Vyner Brooke*: the *Mata Hari* was run down by a Japanese destroyer, after which its passengers were taken off and transferred to the camp at Muntok.

Originally built for the coolies in the tin mines it comprised a number of windowless stone buildings or blocks with sleeping space consisting of raised concrete platforms sloping towards a central passageway, and at the far end a small room with a tap and water tank for bathing and another room with a row of squatting type latrines. More and more people kept arriving — a large number of British and Dutch servicemen, also many Dutch and Eurasian families.

That first night we lay on cold concrete slabs trying to sleep — the small children screamed all night and every hour a Jap guard tramped through our block and seemed to take a delight in hitting our shins with the butt end of his rifle. Fortunately this only happened the first few nights, but the mosquitos were a constant nuisance.

There were 5 doctors in the camp, 2 of them women, and at this time there were 6 British Nursing Sisters and a few Chinese nurses. Then 25 Australian Army Sisters joined us. We took it in turns to help with the wounded and the guardroom was turned into a surgery. The doctors had a few drugs with them.

21 FEBRUARY 1942. A British Air Force officer had to have a foot amputated. Alice Rossie and I assisted the surgeon who had to do it in a most primitive manner. The Japs refused to let the patient go to the local hospital or to send in the right instruments, so someone made a saw out of a knife. It was just as well this poor man, Armstrong, was too ill to know what was happening. Another man had been bayonetted in the stomach when trying to get a drink of water. One

day this man was lying on the surgery floor waiting to have his dressing done when the Jap guard came in and ground his heel into the man's wound.

One night we were called up to attend to another group of people just brought in. They had been on board the *Kuala*. The survivors had clung to the rafts and some were burnt black with the sun. One such girl was brought in, the only survivor from a raft full of people. Her eyes were sunk into the back of her head and it was some minutes before we realised she was English. This was Margot Turner, a QA[2] She had reached a small island and after three days there she was taken off by a cargo boat which was in turn sunk the same night. Four days later she was picked up by a Jap battleship and she had survived all this time by collecting rain water in the lid of her powder compact. Margot was much liked by everyone and years later became Matron-in-Chief — Dame Margot Turner.

28 FEBRUARY 1942. I was in the surgery that afternoon when 2 people were brought in: one a tall Australian Army Nursing Sister called Vivian Bullwinkel, the other a British Army Soldier. Both were covered with scratches and septic mosquito bites. Vivian had had a terrible experience. She had been with 22 other Australian sisters on rafts trying to reach the shore, they waded towards the beach and landed near the town of Muntok. The Australian sisters joined some other people on the beach; these included elderly civilians and servicemen, some of them were wounded.

[2] A member of Queen Alexandra's Imperial Military Nursing Service.

They all spent the night on the beach then the next day some of the civilians and servicemen decided to walk towards Muntok to find help. The Australian sisters stayed with the wounded. Soon a number of Japanese soldiers appeared, they made the men walk a little distance away beyond the rocks, then proceeded to machine gun and bayonet them to death. The Japs then returned to the Australian girls and made them form up in a line and told them to walk into the sea, then proceeded to shoot them in the back. They were all killed except Vivian who lay down pretending to be dead. After the Japs had gone she wandered through the jungle for 10 days. She came across the British soldier on the first day, he was one of the men who had been bayonetted but survived; he died in the camp a few days later. They eventually reached a village where the Japs found them and brought them to join us. Miss Jones, the senior Australian sister, was told about this shooting of the 22 Australian sisters, and it was decided not to tell the other Australian sisters as it would have upset them so much to hear the fate of their friends.

Twice a day we were given a small bowl of rice with a little thin vegetable soup. The first few days we also had weak tea in the early morning but afterwards we only had a cup of hot water. Once we had a small amount of stewed dried octopus with our rice, which made a change. Dysentery developed and most people had swollen ankles. There were an increasing number of flies and no disinfectant. Armstrong, the Air Force Officer, had to have his other foot amputated — he was very brave and never complained — mercifully he died a few days later. Soon after, another man died of dysentery.

After the surrender of Singapore Mrs de Moubray spent a short time in the Katong internment camp before joining a march to Changi, the military cantonment at the eastern end of the island of Singapore which the Japanese turned into a jail for white prisoners of war and civilians.

On the 8th March we went to Changi. Most of the camp walked the 9 miles there, but I had conveniently hit my leg with the axe when chopping wood. I had no pain, but it began to ache when humping baggage from our house to the road, where the Nips were providing transport for our effects. It was also oozing through the elastoplast, and the doctors said that it might become very nasty if I did the march. I went on the last but one conveyance.

It gave me a ghastly impression going to the door of one of the cells — a sort of mortuary cement slab in the middle of it, bare walls, and the barred window right up at the top. I couldn't help remarking "And to think that we even imprisoned Chinese criminals in such places!"

Also on the march to Changi was a nurse, Gladys Tompkins, who has left a detailed memoir of the time she spent there, dictated at the age of eighty-two when she had lost her sight. An amateur artist, she was able to see the prison from a different viewpoint and this helped her to survive.

At first, at night from one of the outside exercising

yards, the prison, with every cell lighted, looked like a beautiful ship alongside a wharf. Gradually the bulbs disappeared, and after the first few months most of the prison was in darkness. The bulbs were taken by the men to help in the construction of radios. . . .

The camp was very well run. Everyone was supposed to do some small job of work, although those over fifty could be excused if they wished. A few did wish to be exempt, and some under fifty also had a pain or an ache which enabled them to get out of work. The camp certainly brought out the best or the worst in people. The amusing part was that in 1944, when the Nips decided to pay us 25 or 30 cents a day for our work, or when the workers were given a little extra rice, then a few found they were not too ill or weak to do a small job.

A Red Cross shop was organised and was opened for an hour each day, and was a very important adjunct to our life in the camp. Mrs Mulvaney's efforts to open a barter shop were a wonderful help too. It started with her telling us to make something and sell it. My first effort was using a ball of string to crochet a sponge bag, with a coconut shell in the bottom, to hold a flannel, soap and toothbrush.

One day we were notified that there would be an issue of eggs. The notice said that anyone who had a bad egg could have it replaced. I bought an egg for 12 cents. It looked like water, and I showed it to several in the Crypt who agreed it was bad. I then showed it to the Assistant Store-keeper, who did not think it SMELT bad, and said I must show it to the Storekeeper. Later in the day I was told I must also show the shell, which had been thrown away. This was now Saturday and they announced that if the egg was bad I must show the egg on Monday to get it replaced. So over I went to the store on Monday, and was told I must take it up to the office. On arriving there I was told I must show the shell. However, I was allowed to throw away the bad egg safely screwed in a bottle and was PROMISED another. The next egg I bought was also bad, so I carefully bottled the egg and was then told again that it could not be replaced unless I could show the shell too.

The third bad egg was shown through the same procedure, except the Storekeeper told me to show it to one of the kitchen staff. She said she was now quite willing to take my word for it! She was so sick of looking and smelling bad eggs that she could not bear the sight of another one.

The water tap had become an important conversation spot, and there a friend said that she had had a bad egg. I told her to count her blessings as I already had had three! Although this was such a small incident it showed how important food was in all our minds.

At the end of the first six months, all women and children signed "under duress" a Jap oath to the effect that they would not try to escape. One refused, but the Japs said it did not matter! Sullivan, a big Irish girl, took out her pen to sign, and then calmly filled her pen in the Nip's ink. The Nip said "that is stealing", to which she replied "You said it — I am in the right place!" . . .

As I was able to take a very good box of paints and a drawing block into internment I spent a lot of my time painting. My chief subject on paper was the papayas which we had grown, and whatever else appealed to me. Various women said "Why make the place look so attractive?" Also, I painted the mosquito nets out in the moonlight, and anything that I thought was picturesque or worth recording. The effect of light and shade in some parts of the prison was interesting. There was a remarkable chimney, and the cloud effects behind this chimney were very spectacular. I also did sketches of the prison from different points of view, some of which I sold, and designs which I gave to various people to embroider on pieces of cloth. My interest in painting and gardening was a God-send to me.

The cloud effects and sunsets seen over the prison walls were very beautiful, and a great delight. Many people sat outside to watch the stars, and at times we thought we saw the Southern Cross. It was something the Japanese could not take away from us.

The women were very good at putting on shows. How ingenious women can be! Mrs Palomar, whose family ran a circus, was helpful at this and organised one for us. The top half of the tallest lady in the world, with a midget beside her; the orang-outang was very well portrayed, and the fattest woman in the world; one exhibit was half man, half woman, with someone else as a bearded lady, while others were clowns. The horse trainer looked very handsome in circus costume with the seal trainer, dogs et cetera. This circus of Mrs Palomar's was exceedingly good and we were permitted to show it to the men, in the main courtyard, although no communication was allowed.

The Japanese had a clever way with their mental torture. Rumours went around that we were to be shot, or that something else would happen to us, none of which ever occurred, but these rumours always produced a degree of tension. About once a week two Japanese used to come in, always after our five o'clock evening bun, when many people were down in the carpenter's shop playing bridge or other games. One of them we named "Bluesocks" and we never discovered whether he was drunk or drugged, but when he came he bellowed about nothing and kicked over anything that was near, and on one occasion two women were each given a crack on the head. All this would last about ten minutes. As it was regularly done we eventually took it in our stride and found out afterwards that something like this occurred in the camps in Borneo and other places. We learned, too, that most of the guards were Koreans who were especially trained to run internment camps. The Sikhs[3] and Nips came round the prison at all hours of the day and night, shuffling, in large boots, and carrying rifles with fixed bayonets, the idea being to prevent us from having a good night's rest. However, it reached a rather ludicrous stage when people during the night were asked to bow if they were awake! It was sad, too, to see our five foot eight, to six foot tall men bowing to the little "squibs" of Japanese who did not even come up to their shoulders. It brought tears to one's eyes.

[3] Indian soldiers captured by the Japanese who joined the "Indian Nationalist Army".

Another nurse, Maria de Jonge, was the daughter of a former Governor of the Dutch East Indies. On the outbreak of war she was Matron-in-Charge of the First General Alfred Hospital at Bandoeng in western Java. She was not interned but allowed to return to Batavia, where in June 1942 she joined an underground Resistance movement, providing medical help, and later arms, to soldiers and Resistance fighters in hiding. Eventually, the organization was penetrated by the Japanese and Maria de Jonge found herself a prisoner of the Kempei-tai, the equivalent of the Gestapo. She later described this harrowing experience, and her subsequent internment and court-martial, in measured terms whose underlying stoicism and humour hint at the great courage of this remarkable woman.

The Kempei-tai was installed in a big Roman Catholic school, a very long, low house with a large garden at the back. How often I had passed it on a bicycle and even lived in the street which ran along the garden.

When we drove in at eleven o'clock at night everything was dark in the large bare hall except for a small light on the guard's table. It had been completely silent; as we entered there was suddenly a lot of noise. Japanese running about, doors banging, shouting. I stood in front of the guard's table, feeling very lonesome.

After a long wait I was taken into a room on the right of the central hall, where I was allowed to sit down in a corner which boasted four chairs and a small round table. Three Japanese sat down with me. A quick look round showed nothing frightening; I saw no sticks or other instruments of torture; obviously it was not one of the rooms reserved for that purpose; too

175

much furniture and too near the central hall.

My impression was correct. It was a rather formal questioning regarding name, age, education, marriage etc.

My questioner was a fairly young man, small, slender, rather good-looking, with a broad smooth flat, cleanshaven face, but merciless slit eyes. His name I discovered only much later, for no names of the Japanese were ever mentioned. Safety first! This fellow conducted the whole investigation of our group and I was often questioned by him again, but though I several times heard tales of his cruelty, I never had any personal experience.

After about an hour of this, I was led away to the cells. . . . Again I was searched, everything in my pockets was taken out except a handkerchief. After much begging I was allowed to take my second uniform-coat to use as pillow. Fortunately they did not take my hairpins and comb out of my long hair. Having been thus examined from head to foot, I was pushed into cell 7 and for the first time in my life found myself behind lock and key. It was an abominable sensation.

With the exception of four sleeping figures rolled in a blanket there was absolutely nothing to see. Four blank walls scribbled all over by my predecessors; high up one small barred window; in the corner something that looked like a big square stone block through which, closer inspection revealed, ran a deep gutter and proved at once to be the lavatory. That was all. A lamp in the ceiling, which was on day and night.

Two of the four sleepers stirred and I saw two heads

for a moment peeping out of the blankets.

"Hallo", said a sleepy female voice, "just come in?"

"Yes."

"Bad luck. Better go to sleep. You are not allowed to sit or stand at night, except on the throne". (This obviously meant the stone block in the corner. A good name!)

I spread one of the blankets that I had received before going in, on the floor and laid down under the second one. Bandoeng is considerably less hot than the towns in the plains and the tiles were chilly, for no sun ever penetrated in the cells. Shoes had been taken away; we had to walk about on bare feet.

After ten minutes the small of my back ached intolerably, so did my shoulder and hipbones, but strange to say after some time I did fall into a light sleep, still completely dazed by the events of the past few hours and trying not to think what the morning might bring. . . .

6.30. All the inmates of the cells were sitting on their haunches before the low doors awaiting breakfast. Making any sort of toilet was impossible. There was one drinking bowl in the cell, that could, with infinite trouble, be partly filled with water which occasionally ran through the gutter of the lavatory when the guards felt like opening the taps. In this we could dip our fingers and dampen our faces. No soap, no towel, no toothbrush, no comb, except the one in my hair, which was of course promptly used by everybody; but I drew the line at the Javanese, who were so full of lice, one could see them walk about. The idea that I too would soon have them made me shudder. But it was as well to get used to the idea. By the time it was a fact (within a week) it quite belonged to the scheme of things.

Breakfast! Along came two native boys superintended by the cook, sometimes a Chinese, sometimes a Japanese. They carried two objects looking like tables with very short legs. On the one were plates of rice, on the other something that was supposed to be a *sajoer*. Ordinarily this is a kind of souplike dish that can be prepared in endless variety with vegetables, fish, shrimps, curry, coconut, meat and all sorts of tasty ingredients typical of the country. So this name was far too dignified for the half raw leeks cooked in saltless water to which was added some sort of Chinese foodstuff which gave off a sickly sweet smell.

One representative from each cell was allowed to come out and collect the bowls and plates for himself and his cellmates. Fascinated I watched the lynx-eyes with which they swiftly examined each plate and bowl and quickly picked out the ones they thought held most. Often there was a difference, for the food was obviously carelessly divided and then the last ones had the worst of it. Poor fellows! It did not make much difference for mostly there was very little of anything, although that too varied sometimes. With this food came bowls of very weak sugarless tea, which was in any case clean and refreshing.

It was an unappetising breakfast, but we all ate it and after ten minutes had to hand in the bowls and plates again.

After this event the natives came along with pails of water, floor cloths and brooms and every group had to clean its own cell. After that two or three of the women had to clean the corridor. We liked that, for, bent double with the wet floorcloth, we had to pass all the cells and could see who were in it and sometimes exchange a few words. If one got caught by an unpleasant guard, kicks and blows were the result, but we didn't mind that much and tried again every time.

At eight o'clock the office started work and we sat again in front of the door to see who came in and went to the guards table to fetch some unhappy prisoner or other.

Sometimes an interpreter came along, sometimes a Kempei official. For the first time I saw some of the professional torturers. Brrr . . . what an unpleasant-looking lot they mostly were, although that was not always true for a few of the blandest, most non-commital looking ones were the worst. I wondered which one of this horrible group was coming to fetch me and who would be my questioner.

My cellmates had told me that things were much better than they used to be, as the new commandant was a comparatively humane sort of person. To him, amongst other things, were due the blankets and the regular cleaning of the cells. But the cleaning of the prisoners themselves had not yet occurred to anybody.

Whilst chatting about one thing and another, as is usual between oldtimers and a newcomer, the Eurasian girl suddenly said: "That's for you; an interpreter." And indeed the guard fetched the key and opened the door.

Upstairs were the torture-rooms. The broad low staircase drew my eye irresistibly. But no, we turned left and marched along a number of offices and entered one of them, luxuriously furnished. A large, beautiful writing desk in a corner on the left near the window; four roomy easy chairs round a table on the right. Nobody there.

"Sit down" said my guide, pointing to one of the chairs. This seemed queerly polite treatment, but I sat down and waited. What next. Not two minutes later a clout on the head and several blows in my face from behind completely took me by surprise, as it was meant to do.

"Get up, you bitch, how dare you go and sit in a chair!"

I got up and turned. Two Japanese strangers, were standing behind me.

"I was told to by the guide who brought me here, sir."

"*Bohong*![4] Sit on the floor".

I had to kneel, stretch my feet out straight and sit on my heels. Try that for five minutes and see what it feels like.

Suddenly heavy steps, a loud voice, and in strode an officer. "Get up and bow, can't you," snapped one of my companions.

I looked at my surroundings and back at the officer, who was treated with considerable respect. It must be the commandant himself and this was of course his office, hence the luxury.

So it proved to be. He subsided into one of the easy chairs. An interpreter sat down in another.

"Sit down."

[4] Malay for liar.

I went down on the floor in my former position. The interpreter got up and fetched a really imposing stick, thinned down at one end into a handle in order to make it possible to grasp and there we were.

Except the beginning I remember very little of this first cross-examination. It was long and painful. . . .

Answering questions was on the whole not so bad. Most of the people I had worked with had been in prison a long time already and I could say anything I wanted about them. I stuck to the policy of always speaking the truth, or else by saying: "I don't know." It was the best thing to do. Lies were dangerous, for they wrote everything down and if you are questioned about thirty times in a few weeks, sometimes three times a day, as I was, there is no hope of remembering the twelfth time what you have said the first or third or sixth time. They checked every statement and if you were found out it merely led to trouble.

At last, after long and weary hours, I went back to the cell. My cellmates were very sympathetic and also very curious, for life was dull and they wanted to know everything and I was undressed to examine the damage. It looked pretty bad, but no serious harm had been done and a month later practically no trace of it was left.

To my surprise and relief I was never beaten again except by the guards when they were out of temper. To what I owed this leniency, I don't know. It was obviously by order of the commandant, but they tried every other trick they could think of. . . .

There was one guard who always made an awful lot of noise and threatened everybody with death and damnation, but I never saw him hit anybody and at night, when nobody, not even his colleague was there, he came along with a huge kettle of steaming, sweetened coffee and all the prisoners got a glassfull. That everybody had to drink out of the same glass was a detail that did not worry us, and it was the only sugar we ever received.

I had now been at the Kempei for two months, the others longer. We had never washed, either our bodies, our hair, our teeth or our clothes. There was simply nothing to do it with.

Then, one day, I was again called to the commandant's office, who, at a given moment evidently meaning to be funny, asked me how I liked his hotel. There was still plenty of fight in me. I exploded and told him in all the most colourful English and Malay words that I could think of what I thought of it. He seemed considerably surprised at my vehemence, but to my astonishment instead of being duly (and not unjustly) punished for this lack of decorum, he inquired what were the worst conditions in my opinion.

Now I in my turn was stunned, but overcoming my surprise answered that the dirtiness of our persons, the insufficient food and the dullness of doing nothing for fourteen hours a day were all equally bad.

He said nothing and after a time I was taken back to the cell. Then in the afternoon, shortly after the lunch hour, we suddenly saw a rare and exciting sight. A guard walked along the corridor with three large pieces of Sunlight soap in his hand, which he put down on the table. Now began one of the most amusing scenes in which it has been my privilege to take part.

Three Japanese soldiers put bayonets on their rifles and the women's cells were opened. There were eight of us. We were ordered out and marched through the corridor and a side-door to the back of the building and out into the garden. Oh, the sensation of being in the open air! It was quite lovely weather, the grass felt soft and warm under our bare feet, the trees were so green and the air so mild; we suddenly realised *how* utterly appalling, chilling and lifeless the cells were.

We had fortunately little time to reflect upon these things. We walked along through the grounds to a stable situated right at the back where several good-looking horses stood chewing contentedly. I could have kissed them. Next to this stable stood a high contrivance of waterpipes to which were attached three or four douches. Arriving there we were ordered to strip, we were handed a piece of soap and a couple of tiny towels and were told to bathe. The three armed Japanese carefully posted themselves around us. After all, we might try to escape!

One of the women said to me: "Look here, we can't do this, with the guards a few yards away and right in the open air in full view of the main building."

"Well," I answered, "perhaps you can't, but I can. I haven't seen a drop of water for over two months and I'm going to wash every inch of myself and my clothes if they give us time enough."

And they did, that first time. In less than a minute eight stark-naked women, tall ones, short ones, dark ones, light ones, thin ones and plump ones, were having the wash of their lives in the middle of the garden!

We laid our clothes to dry on the grass and wandered about naked. The guards gave us a cigarette, occasionally prodded the fence with their bayonets to prevent people on the road trying to peep through and were completely undisturbed by such a display of naked femininity. In their own country they are used to mixed bathing; they think nothing of it. When one of the women once said to a guard that she felt shy and embarrassed, he looked at her in genuine astonishment and asked "Shy? Whatever for?"

By the summer of 1944 Maria de Jonge was being held in a prison at Tjipinang, housed in a filthy, verminous cell and fed on the crudest offal until the end of October, when she was sent to a court-martial at Koenigsplein and sentenced to five years' imprisonment. Conditions at Tjipinang inevitably led to disease.

One day a dysentery epidemic broke out in the prison. It was appalling. Ten to fifteen deaths a day for weeks on end was quite normal. The stench from the hospital, where hundreds of patients were just lying in the corridors and on the open field in their own filth, was nauseating. The Dutch dentist did a wonderful job of work as far as he could. At last he fell ill himself, but recovered. When we had to go to the hospital for treatment, we were green before we arrived there. But in the women's block only one woman, an old native, caught the disease and died from it.

As the months went by the food became gradually worse. A few things disappeared from the menu and cheaper things were substituted. One of these looked like rasped and dried cocoanut, only it wasn't the genuine article, but the offal thereof. Pig's fodder in fact. This went through the *sajoer* and was supposed to be nourishing. The results were indescribable. To say that it worked like a laxative was far too mild. The food came out as quickly as it went in and one could eat the whole day without any discomfort, except for the fact that one was always hungry. It was so bad, that even when eating it was not possible to sit through a meal lasting a quarter of an hour and it became quite normal for one of the company to sit on her haunches above the hole, while the others cheerfully went on eating not three yards away.

The only meat we ever got was lungs, stomachs, intestines and suchlike, practically uncleaned, just cooked. It was the only thing which I was totally unable to eat, although a good many people were quite keen on it. The men, who were less well fed than we were, were not so squeamish and were glad when they could get it. Besides this they ate rats (which taste quite good I've been told), cats and anything else they could get hold of.

As the end of the war approached Maria de Jonge was moved to a camp in central Java. After the atom bomb raids on the cities of Hiroshima and Nagasaki the Japanese surrendered on 15 August 1945. In the last agonizing weeks of waiting Maria de Jonge lived "between hope and despair, between bursts of energy and lassitude", and always with the fear that her captors might kill their prisoners rather than yield them up to the victorious Allies.

The months slipped by and it became more and more noticeable that matters were not turning out as the

Japanese had hoped and expected. How overjoyed we were to hear of the capitulation of Germany and the end of the war in Europe. But hope faded when we heard that Churchill had made a speech in which he said that the war in the Pacific might still last a long time, perhaps years. The news from the Pacific front did not sound too hopeful as far as it penetrated to us. We had no maps to follow the progress of the Allies. Bataan, Corregidor, Leyte and many other well-known names could not be exactly located. We had to go by the unreliable rumours that trickled into the prison and for the rest by what we saw and noticed around us. Sometimes we managed to steal a newspaper from the office and Yashima[5], without ever saying anything definite, or rather, not saying anything at all, yet managed to give us hints that things were not going so well.

The forewoman[6] and I spent several nights outside the cells during alarms that lasted for hours. Only twice anything really happened. Once a batch of planes flew over evidently bound for other goals, machine-gunning a bit on the way, dropping a bomb or two far away from us and once there was regular bombardment on the port of Semarang. It was a fairly severe attack that shook the walls of our abode. The planes came back again and again. The forewomen and I watched wholly fascinated. We had seen very little of this sort of thing and the lights that were thrown out followed

---

[5] The camp commandant.

[6] A native woman appointed as a kind of "trusty", responsible for inmates.

by the heavy booms which sounded quite near, the airblasts, some of which nearly threw us off our feet, were no mean thrill. But it was very disagreeable for all the others who were locked up and nearly went frantic. The natives all huddled together like animals, silent and terrified. In the European blocks there was occasionally a lot of noise through somebody having hysterics, while others chattered and made jokes to forget that it was not at all impossible that a bomb might easily fall a mile or so out of radius and create havoc amongst all these trapped human beings. However as far as we were concerned nothing else happened and the next day we were all duly at our work again and ordinary routine continued, only interrupted by the air alarms that sent every one back to their cells. We of course expected a lot more to happen, but for us the excitement was over.

And what would happen if the Allies invaded Java? Several Japanese had already said long ago that, if such were to be the case, all Europeans would be killed. If they were going to stay long enough, all women in the camps would be sent to Borneo to the mines. The plans were all ready.

And so, between hope and despair, between bursts of energy and lassitude we lived our daily, outwardly monotonous routine into August. During the second week our commandant suddenly began to drop veiled hints. Less than half words. Nothing was said. But we, who knew literally and symbolically how to feed on practically nothing, pricked up our ears and tried to steal the Malay paper from the guard's office every evening.

187

At last one evening we were rewarded and we read about the atomic bombs dropped on Nagasaki and Hiroshima. Events followed quickly in the shape of the proclamation of the republic of Indonesia (which did not mean anything to us) and shortly after that the capitulation of Japan.

The war was over!

CHAPTER
SEVEN

Front Line Nurses

Before the war Syria had been under the control of the French, who exercised a League of Nations mandate. In June 1940 the French High Commissioner in Syria came out in support of the Vichy government in France, and in 1941 the country became a refuelling stop for German military aircraft en route to Iraq, which from April power was held by a military junta in the pay of Germany.

To prevent a possible German occupation, British and Free French forces under General Maitland Wilson and General Catroux invaded the country. After five weeks of heavy fighting the Free French took control of Syria.

At the beginning of May 1941, the Hadfield Spears Front Line Surgical Unit arrived at Suez after a long voyage via South Africa on the troopship *Otranto*. Their original destination had been Port Sudan, but they were re-routed to Dera in southern Syria, near the Jordanian border, where they caught up with the fighting.

Josephine Pearce recalls the harsh conditions the unit endured.

The Vichy had blown up all the wells but one. There was a little Convent of French and Arab Sisters of St

Joseph and the diminutive Rev. Mother had sat firmly on her Well, spreading her skirts out and refusing to get off, telling the Vichy officer that he must blow her up. He had to retreat, so that well was saved.

We put up our tents, well spaced, and some of us slept over a cesspool. I received a septic bite from one of the filthy mosquitoes. We were perpetually being machine-gunned by Vichy planes. We nurses would rush across the desert to be with our wounded and as we ran machine gun bullets spattered all round us, but not one of us was hit.

Our work was heavy at Dera for as well as the Free French wounded we learned later that our little band had dealt with one third of the British wounded in that sector. Our surgeons operated all night. We would go among the rows of stretchers picking out those who might be saved. So many died before we could find time to help them.

As the reader will know, children who had nannies were with them far more than their parents. Young English officers did not die calling for their mothers, no, it was "Nanny, where are you?" We would reassure them letting them believe we were the nannies and so they died peacefully holding our hands murmuring "Nanny don't leave me".

Sleep during the day was almost impossible. The flies loved my tent so much that I made them a present of it and at the Rev. Mother's invitation I put a mattress on a table in the nuns' little school. There I was not constantly dodging bullets and flies plus virulent mosquitoes.

Nazareth British Military Hospital was the Base

hospital. They sent a message to ask who we were, who sent the cases in such good condition, perfect operations encased in plaster and not needing to be touched for three months. Colonel Fruchaud had adopted this method during the Spanish war and the wounds were packed with Septoplex.

Our position was becoming untenable at Dera. The railway was now blown up and the British were fighting back. We packed up and moved on to Damascus. What memories of St Paul's journey. Blindness and conversion passed before my mind. He must have seen it just as we did, for that ancient city was already old then.

General Catroux was in charge of the forces in that area under General de Gaulle. Madame Catroux came to us one day in a great state of agitation. She had found some Free French wounded in a Vichy-run hospital. They were kept on dirty mattresses and untended by their own countrywomen (nuns at that). Madame Catroux had sent sheets, blankets, dressings and pillows but these had been used for the Vichy wounded only. Colonel Fruchaud sent some nurses . . .

We arrived at a large French hospital run by nuns. The Vichy were cared for and then we found putrid skeletons on dirty mattresses, some crying for water. I have never spoken to a nun as I did to that French Rev. Mother. Her explanation, which was that she had to obey orders, drew my reply, "Did you vow to be a bride of Christ or the Vichy"? "Would Christ have left these men in such a state?" We got those poor men away. The wounds were full of maggots so that I had to use a spoon to remove them from their wounds. These maggots were actually helping drain out the wounds. We bathed the men and put them in our sheets and blankets. Their amazement and gratitude was touching.

In January 1942 the Spears Hadfield unit arrived in a more important theatre of war, the Western Desert.

Since the winter of 1940-1 the war in North Africa had flowed back and forth along the Mediterranean coastline. To the south the desert yielded nothing, so campaigning resolved itself into a contest for the chain of small ports of supply on the Mediterranean coast. Cut off from these, an army was quickly deprived of water, fuel, ammunition, food and reinforcements which, in that order, were the essentials of desert warfare.

The Hadfield Spears unit was bound for Tobruk, a key port on the Libyan coast. It had been captured from the Italians by the British in January 1941 and then unsuccessfully besieged by Rommel's Afrika Korps. It was relieved in November 1941 by the British, who forced Rommel back to Benghazi. In the summer of 1942 Rommel launched a new, successful offensive which took Tobruk on 21 June. The city changed hands for the last time during Montgomery's advance after the second Battle of El Alamein.

We arrived at a camp in the Sinai Desert at 7 pm. Our heavy convoy was there. There was only one small tent and two little huts. The Australian boys turned out a hut for us, it was very sweet of them. Being us, we have of course struck the worst night they have had. It rained, it blew sand and the roof of our abode nearly blew away. We were smothered in sand. . . .

We quickly realised the importance of our thick

men's underwear and battle dress for the Western desert was so cold at night that we slept on our camp beds with every article of clothing on. Combs to our ankles, three pairs of socks, desert boots, warm feminine underwear over the combs plus khaki jerseys, full battle dress, woollen scarves and greatcoats. With all this we squeezed into our sleeping bags and then we froze all night.

They moved up through the desert, travelling as far as they could each day past the gutted hulks of German and British tanks. Sometimes they were unable to pitch their tents because the soil was so rocky; sandstorms blew up and there were uncharted minefields.

Convoys passed us in both directions and the expressions on the men's faces at seeing women so very far up is never to be forgotten. At last we saw Tobruk with its magnificent natural harbour and our 300-mile journey seemed at an end. On arrival we were mistaken for a travelling ENSA[1] unit! how we all laughed, but the Town Major was horrified and turned us out into the desert as he said it was not safe for us. He did not know that we never thought of safety. Finally we were put up at a beach hospital by the seashore three miles out of Tobruk. We had real beds and water to wash in.

We were surrounded with guns; the famous ack-ack[2] of Tobruk, the little Naval craft in the harbour were constantly being sunk. These were captured

[1] Entertainments National Service Association; its primary role was to entertain the forces.
[2] Anti-aircraft artillery.

yachts used for reconnaisance work by the Navy.

One night strictly against rules, we had a party aboard a converted Greek yacht. This little boat still had its piano. I do not know if the reader has ever been below water level in a craft while ack-ack guns are being fired all round. It sounds like hundreds of shod feet stamping above your head. Suddenly there was some extra noise, and coming down the gangway was an officer and I think two men. Their little craft next to ours had just been sunk! They joined the party and the piano was played very loudly and we all sang while the row above us lasted.

The Hadfield Spears unit was then ordered to Tmimi, 50 miles west of Tobruk.

The next day we were in our cars, our long convoy behind, the mobile mattress steriliser doing its work, the truck with the autoclave was doing its work with the dressing drums — all as we moved, for we were very well equipped and the envy of the British Medical Corps.

As we drove along, we noticed that all the British convoys were going back towards Egypt while the French were going in the opposite direction. Were they ignoring British orders again? It looked very much to us as if we were going against an army in full retreat! We were more and more sure that we were going in the wrong direction. We muttered under our breath, "More like a defeat than victory", and we wondered what on earth we were doing. Then there were no more troops passing us. We were nearing escarpments —

tall rocky hillocks of grey stone. The evening shades of orange and mauve gave them such beauty.

Suddenly we were ordered to stop in a vast open space. They called it Tmimi. Here we had to have one large tent pitched for a ward. We had to lay many white sheets on the ground. Some had already been dyed red to form a gigantic Red Cross to be seen from the air. It was supposed to protect the hospital but the enemy were using ambulances to convey arms and, in one case, girls were brought to isolated German units. One ambulance captured by the British on its way back to Derna had not only girls but a shamefaced General! They had vast quantities of silk stockings and Nivea cream, some of which was passed on to us later.

But to return to Tmimi. There was water so the sisters stripped and we were in the midst of a glorious wash when a soldier put his head through the tent flap, causing much squealing from naked women!

"Get your clothes on and get into your cars at once." It was an English voice. "You can't remain here. Rommel will be here any moment and this spot has been earmarked for a battle." We had to rush, the equipment would be seen to for us, we must get back to Tobruk at once. . . .

Just after our return to Tobruk, Colonel Fruchaud took Nancy, our theatre sister, and Michael, a young Quaker,[3] up to the front with the mobile theatre. As Michael and Nancy were walking across the desert pitted with shell holes, a plane came lower and Michael

---

[3] The Quakers' faith prevented them from actually fighting, although they could serve as non-combatants.

just had time to shout "Nancy, jump into that shell hole", when the plane deliberately dropped a bomb. It was a direct hit. Hardly anything of this brave young man of 21 was found. Back at the Beach, the Quakers held a meeting. These are not funerals as we know them. Those of us who could joined them in a tent, our priest as well. All sit around and silence reigns; they are thinking of occasions in his life they best remember. Someone says something he remembers, then silence while we meditate and then someone else would speak about him. This went on for some time the night after he was killed and the Catholic priest remembered Michael's cheerful acceptance of all dangers.

At this time we noticed on our walks by the rocky inlet with some wounded, that under the desert rocks there peeped out the tiniest flowers, bright red anemones, little crocuses, all so very small and this started a kind of rehabilitation caused by nature for these men who had seen so much horror. We collected flowers in cigarette tins and then sent them to Kew Gardens. We even had bully beef tins on our mess tent table with flowers in them.

In February 1943 Josephine Pearce left Suez for an eventful unescorted voyage to England. By the time she reached home, the tide of war had turned. The Afrika Korps was in full retreat after being defeated at the second Battle of El Alamein. On the Eastern Front, even before the surrender of the encircled German 6th Army at Stalingrad in January 1943, the Red Army had launched a massive counter-attack to regain the territories lost in the summer of 1942. The strategic initiative was passing to the Allies.

196

However, in the west another sixteen months of preparation lay ahead before the invasion of Europe. On D-Day, 6 June 1944, the Allies launched Operation Overlord, the invasion of Normandy. On 12 June the last gap in the Allied line, between Omaha and Utah beaches, was closed, linking their forces together in a beach-head 42 miles long.

That night the first two women to land in Normandy came ashore on Juno beach near the town of Courseulles-sur-Mer. They were Iris Ogilvie and Mollie Giles, Sisters in Princess Mary's Royal Air Force Nursing Service and members of No. 50 Mobile Field Hospital, 83 Group, RAF.

Personal tragedy had set Iris on the road to Normandy.

Several months before, I had written to the then Matron-in-Chief of the Princess Mary's RAF Nursing Service indicating that I wished to serve in a Mobile Field Hospital being prepared for the Invasion. I was fully aware that the possibility of this was questionable. My husband, Donald, a Squadron Leader flying bombers, had been killed in a daylight sortie over Holland. I wanted desperately to make some contribution.

One day, when I was on duty in an RAF Orthopaedic Unit at Loughborough, I was informed by the commanding officer that I had been posted to some location in the South of England and would be receiving further detailed instructions from the Air Ministry. It was not until many weeks later that I realised I had been on trial, being vetted for my suitability. I had no idea of this on my arrival, neither did I know that among the Medical orderlies there was a great deal of hostility to my posting to the unit. When they first heard that a Nursing Sister was to join

197

them, the general opinion was to put it bluntly "We don't want any b— women in this outfit."

However, after three weeks Iris felt that she really belonged to her new unit, "We left our winter quarters in March 1944 and became a Mobile Field Hospital in every sense of the word. I witnessed complete tent camouflage and maintenance, took part in convoy journeys night and day. We had our own transport, electric power, field telephone system, water supplies, cooking facilities and signals unit. We lacked nothing in the way of medical supplies available at the time, operating theatre, X-Ray equipment etc. We even had our own dental unit".

On 5 June Iris joined a convoy to the Concentration Centre at Old Sarum, the first stage in the journey to the Normandy beaches.

I soon joined my friend, Mollie, and we walked together to the entrance of one of the camps, where the Commanding Officer was in deep conversation with the Officer-in-Charge, who suddenly saw us and promptly said, "They're not going over are they?" He was soon informed that we were and also tougher than we looked. I had the disadvantage, in this situation, only being five foot two inches and slim with golden curls showing under my tin hat.

"We can't cater for you to have toilet facilities on your own, just the two of you."

I wasn't too worried. I had long since ceased to worry about such trivial matters. . . .

It is difficult to convey the atmosphere of that strange world so long ago. There were thousands of troops and airmen, vehicles of all shapes and sizes, and the hardware of war. The sheer magnitude of the operation seemed to keep any fear away. I don't seem to remember being anxious or frightened. Some of the troops would give Mollie and I inquisitive looks, but the Red Cross arm bands seemed to convey the message.

On the morning of June 8th, officers of various units gathered in groups including our own unit. At one of these sessions I was handed an emergency pack. It was strange how this little pack seemed to bring things home to me. Inside there were different little packets, concentrated porridge, chocolate etc., a piece of chewing gum and a tiny box, which contained a collar stud, which had a compass at one end. I was most intrigued and thought to myself, if I had to depend on that I would probably end up in Germany.

We were then ushered into one of the bigger tents and told, quite calmly, that we would be moving off, in convoy, at midnight, on our journey to the Marshalling Area at Fareham in Hampshire. "Sunshine"[4] told Mollie and I to be in full battle dress by midnight, with tin hats and packs on our backs. This would be our only baggage, strapped on our backs. The important tin plate and "irons" (cutlery), were a priority and a tin mug tied to one of the straps. Very important as far as I was concerned, a little waterproof bag with my Elizabeth Arden make-up, which was all the rage then. I wasn't going to land in Normandy looking a sight! Bright red lipstick did wonders to pull one's face together.

[4] Their CO, Wing Commander Ingram.

We lay on our beds, in full battle dress, with our Red Cross arm bands in position. Just before midnight, we heard footsteps mounting the stairs and a loud knock on the door. When we opened it, a young man, in his despatch rider's uniform, said, "Right off we go." I was standing on the landing when a bedroom door opened and one of the WAAF Officers appeared. She said, "What's all the noise about?" Then she seemed to stare at us in silence. All I said was goodbye. I think at that moment she realised we were off with the troops. She had such a look of astonishment on her face.

From Fareham they were taken in due course to Gosport for embarkation.

The convoy came to a halt in a suburban street to my surprise. It was early, almost the crack of dawn, and I was astonished to find the inhabitants up and about. Some of the occupants of the houses were waving at us from upstairs windows, others were at their front doors and gardens. The kindness of the women was unbounded. They gave tea to the troops, hot water for a shave and some were even asked to their houses and many were provided with breakfast. One woman gave me a tin of peaches, such a treasured possession in the War. I sat on the pavement and ate the contents of the tin with relish. Morale was tremendous, it's something that has to be experienced, words are inadequate. The generosity and kindness of the people did so much. The men remembered and talked about it in the days that followed. . . .

The next thing I knew, I was embarking. It was an incredible feeling. I seemed to go through all the motions automatically. I didn't utter a word, and as far as I can remember, neither did anyone milling around me. Tanks, vehicles and men poured on to the craft at tremendous speed and in no time at all this laden LCT[5] proceeded to take its place in a vast, Normandy bound, convoy. It was June 11th.

There was a never ending convoy of ships and escorting naval vessels. A couple of men started counting aloud, they reached two hundred. The ships seemed to be packed so tightly, one wondered how they could move with safety. I felt strangely elated at the impressiveness of the scene. We stood there silently and then there was a roar of aircraft overhead, twenty fighter aircraft were patrolling the skies. The reassuring noise, of the fighter aircraft escorting, remained with us for all the hours of daylight. . . .

We spent most of our time sitting on the deck. The troops were singing the familiar songs of the War. The most popular, I think, were "We'll Meet Again" and "Run Rabbit Run" and, of course, we joined in from time to time. At one stage, I sat near some sacks of potatoes and helped the cooks with endless peeling. I must have done this worthwhile job for a long time and was rewarded with a continuous flow of hot tea. The call of "grub's up" was greeted with great enthusiasm. The stew and tinned rice pudding was hot and filling. We were fortunate, on this day, that the sea was calm and there was no sea sickness. Others before us had

[5] Landing craft tank.

experienced it very differently.

We lay off the Normandy beaches for what seemed to all of us, an incredibly long time. We could observe considerable shore activity. Throughout this time the sky was filled with Allied aircraft. Fighters could be seen taking off, in clouds of red dust, from a strip near the shore, being immediately attacked by enemy anti-aircraft fire. It was a grim reminder of the fight being waged in the immediate vicinity of the shore, where our Mobile Field Hospital was soon to land. A cruiser, moored nearby throughout this time, engaged enemy shore positions with her six inch guns. After what seemed to be an eternity, "Sunshine" informed us that the tide was suitable for landing. I still wasn't frightened, but the adrenalin was flowing.

Orders were given to disembark, and we were guided down to the lower deck. I remember standing next to Mollie in the dark, on the left side of the lower deck of the LCT, facing the ramp. I felt as though I was inside a monstrous whale, listening to the noises of the vehicles edging their way down the steep ramp to the shore. I couldn't see what was happening in the darkness, but I was very aware of vehicles noisily moving and personnel dashing about. I felt NO emotion, nothing at all, just standing there with my pack on my back looking downwards towards the ramp which I could just about make out in the dark. We didn't speak a word. Suddenly we were told to go. We scrambled down the ramp and the next thing I remember was feeling sand under my feet. I had landed on Juno/Red Beach near Courseulles-sur-Mer, in the pitch darkness on June 12th, 1944. . . .

I suddenly heard a loud voice, almost in my ear, shouting "Where are you off to?" I stopped dead in my tracks. It was one of the beach-masters. I found my voice and said we were with No. 50, Mobile Field Hospital, RAF, making our way to the Assembly Area. He came right up to me looked into my face and said "Good God". By this time we were completely separated from any other members of our unit.

"Follow me" said the beach-master, "I'll take you down here and arrange for a jeep to take you." We had no idea what he meant by "down here", but, after walking a few yards, we found ourselves standing by some concrete steps leading to what appeared to be an underground shelter. We quickly descended and suddenly heard voices of troops. We were given a tremendous welcome. Someone shouted "Watch out Adolph you've had it now!"

Eventually, despite the darkness, noise and confusion, the two nurses were reunited with their colleagues. Then they got to work setting up the field hospital to await the wounded.

It was an emotional moment for us all as a team when the first casualties arrived. The worst, very serious ones indeed, were from the neighbouring Army Casualty Clearing Station. We were to look after them in readiness for their embarkation by sea back to England the next day. Some were a very sorry sight. The Medical Officers, Mollie and I, Medical Orderlies and other personnel, worked non-stop. We were seeing to field dressings, Intra Venous Infusions, giving injections, Morphia and Penicillin mostly. It was a tremendous blessing that we were already using Penicillin in the Services. It was vital to keep infection at bay.

I must have given gallons of hot tea, and fed those who could eat, and got down to the important task of giving urinals and bed pans. We spent as much time as possible talking to them and lighting the odd "fag" for those who were dying for a smoke. My reward was to see smiles on their faces and in their eyes. I know they appreciated any little thing we could do for them. Next morning, the ambulances arrived to take the serious casualties away, to start their journey back to the UK. Little had they realised, when they landed, that they would be revisiting the beaches so soon. On their journey they were being looked after by a Naval Medical Team. Our thoughts were with them and wondering if they would have a safe passage. Enemy gunfire could be heard, as well as gunfire from our naval vessels off shore.

After a few hours, air evacuation of casualties was getting under way. Our unit was to assist in this task, the work demanding surgical intervention in our operating theatre tent, the other tents retaining casualties prior to their evacuation. Mollie and I were to take it in turns to accompany the casualties to the improvised air strip, flattened by the Royal Engineers, and covered with wire meshing.

Just before leaving, a Medical Orderly came up to me and said, "Sister, can you come with me, there is almost a fight in one of the ambulances". I hurried with him, to find two injured Germans on the top stretchers and one British and one Canadian on the bottom stretchers. They were shouting at each other. I didn't know who was most to blame but it was quite a serious situation. As I couldn't speak German I told the other lads, in no uncertain terms, what I thought of them. I felt at that moment better to be cruel to be kind. I pointed to the Red Cross on my arm and told them we were there to look after wounded Germans, as well as them, and made it plain I wasn't having any nonsense. I don't know if the Germans understood, but calm was restored in the ambulance and I was able to leave. The Medical Orderly told me afterwards that he had no further trouble with them.

We were soon on our way, in the long convoy to the air strip, in an area which had been occupied by the enemy less than two days before. When we arrived, I could see clouds of white dust everywhere and there, standing in readiness, was the familiar shape of an RAF Dakota. They were being used as ambulances. Apparently there had been a counter attack when the plane landed and a tank battle was going on in the wood not far from the end of the strip. Although it was now D + 9,[6] that RAF air strip was still a dangerous place. We could hear the thundering noise of guns and overhead whistled shells from warships lying close to shore.

We heard a few days later that a Dakota was hit by flak as it flew out. When it landed in England over seventy flak holes were found in the fuselage, but no one was hurt. Although we could hear gunfire and the

[6] Nine days after D-Day.

205

occasional shell whistling over head, nothing more serious happened to us. I took it in turn with Mollie to make the journey to the air strip for five days. We had assisted in sending back to the UK one thousand and twenty three cases before we were instructed to move again.

Our medical team was to back up the assault and we had to move to Cussy, a distance of twelve miles on the Bayeux-Cherbourg road. I remember the countless activities everywhere as we bumped and jerked along the road. Endless columns of troops, vehicles and stores were still arriving on the beaches. Even by June 15th, three days after our arrival on the beach-head, it is recorded that half a million men and seventy seven thousand vehicles were ashore and in the bridge-head. I think we all felt that it was the biggest experience that could ever happen to us, and the fact that we were all in the same boat had the effect of boosting our morale.

I think the ambulance I was travelling in was about the sixth vehicle in the convoy. As we approached the entrance to the field chosen for the hospital, there was a loud explosion and it was here our convoy had its first casualty. One of our Sergeants, travelling in the first vehicle, was blown up and injured badly, thankfully not killed. The hospital was set up at speed and finally the large Red Cross spread out in the centre. Looking back I think our stay on this site was the most alarming. Gunners were firing and the air became filled with shell fragments, which rained down on the outer canvas of the tents, or to clang and bang on the lorries.

There was torrential rain at times and casualties began to pile up, as it was not possible to evacuate them by air.

One night was particularly noisy, due to the gunfire and shelling, and we were all busy dashing about. I stopped by one of the lads, who was very poorly, lapsing into periods of unconsciousness. I made certain that all was well with the various tubing, then hurried off to do other things. After a little while, I returned to look at him again. This time he had his eyes wide open and said in a perfectly clear voice, "Where's your tin hat? Who do you think you are, a blinking fairy?" I had forgotten I wasn't wearing one. I went to find my hat and hurriedly put it on. I returned to reassure him, to find he had just died. It was an incident that shook me greatly and that I could never forget.

On another occasion, I remember an injured Sergeant suddenly discovering that the patient next to him was a German pilot, badly burnt. To us he was a "serious burns case". The Sgt became very agitated and asked if he could be moved. I could see that he was greatly upset and I knew that we would have to go along with his wishes. Later, he told me, that some members of his family had been killed in a bombing raid in the UK.

We looked after the German pilot for several days. Parts of his body had third degree burns, but his face was superficially affected, although it was completely covered in dressings, like the rest of his body. I could see his eyes watching us through slits in his bandaged face and head. Again it was difficult, not being able to converse in German. I used to smile at him whenever the opportunity arose. I think he had been with us about five days when one of the Medical Officers instructed me to remove his face dressings. I took them off slowly and to my astonishment and joy I could see that the skin was beautifully healed. I asked the orderly to bring me a mirror and held it up, so that the young pilot could see his face. The look of relief on his face was incredible and then the tears started running down his cheeks and he held my hand. One does not forget such precious moments and I felt his sadness when he was evacuated soon afterwards.

"Jerry" was paying the area some attention. There was continuous noise of gunfire and bits of shrapnel fell amongst the tents. When there was a lull and the noises had subsided, we made tracks for our own unit. I was sitting with my companion in a jeep when we passed some troops on the side of the road. I waved to them and one shouted "Front Line Popsie". I didn't know whether to be flattered or insulted! The quick wit of the troops in these terrible conditions was such a tonic.

Soon they were on the move again.

This time it was Camilly, which lay three and a half miles south east of our original site at Cruelly. It's strange, but I seem to remember every detail of this field. Perhaps the fact that we were stuck there during the battle of Caen, makes me remember it so vividly. We could hear the noise of gunfire, or rocket firing Typhoons, or other aircraft milling about in the confined air space of the bridge-head.

One incident nearly spelt disaster to our hospital. A stricken Liberator bomber, from which the crew had baled out, ran amok in the air over the camp, despite efforts by Allied aircraft to shoot it down in a safe locality. I was in one of the large tents, when I heard a terrible noise. The patient near the entrance to the tent was in bad shape, with an Intravenous drip. I left him hurriedly for a few moments, ran outside to see what was happening. I saw the plane circling round, looking as though it was going to crash at any moment. Then I saw the cooks from the field kitchen, one with a saucepan in his hand running down the field. I knew something terrible was about to happen and rushed back into the tent, to find that some of the more mobile patients had put the more seriously ill one on the floor of the tent, drips and all! I stayed with him and he was very alert to everything that was going on. The men outside in the field were very aware that the aircraft was pilotless. It circled menacingly over our hospital for about fifteen minutes, which seemed an eternity, slowly losing altitude and finally crashed in flames within four hundred yards of our camp. What a miracle it was that it didn't crash on our tents.

Mary Mulrey, by now a Sister in Queen Alexandra's Imperial Military Nursing Service, arrived in Normandy only a few days after Iris Ogilvie and Mollie Giles to serve with 101 British General Hospital. She embarked for Normandy on 18 June. The crossing was rough, but "we have not time to be seasick, Sister", said her superior with true British phlegm, pouring her a stiff tot of rum. Disembarking, amid the expected noise of gunfire and exploding ships, required more athletic prowess than it had for Iris Ogilvie.

The sailors had attached a scrambling net to the side of the ship and in theory we were to descend in agile fashion down this net, whilst the sailors on this side helped us over the edge. The men on the landing craft were ready to catch us as we jumped aboard. That was the theory but the heavy seas made the synchronisation of these events highly unlikely. The wearing of a "Mae West", although essential in such weather, would increase our girth and make the effort of climbing down the scrambling net very difficult. It might have been easier if we were all eight months pregnant.

Our strange silhouetted shapes were lit up periodically by the flares as we stood there in fear and trepidation as to who should go first. I volunteered not out of bravery but because of feeling sea-sick again, anything to get off that ship!

I was all right whilst the sailor lowered me over the edge of the deck, and whilst I could feel his strong arms, then I was on my own. I kept going down with "Mae West" bulk constantly pushing me away from the too-mobile scrambling net. I thought I was almost there when a voice behind me said, "Hold on until the exact moment I say and then jump backwards." I was soaked in spray by now, cold, wet and frightened, but when someone shouted "Now" I fell straight back into waiting arms. The sailors on the landing craft were a very jolly bunch, full of jokes and laughter. We were the first English women who had literally fallen into their arms in Normandy!

Matron was the last to come down, which she did without too much loss of dignity.

We clambered aboard a 3 tonner open lorry after

breakfast and set out inland. I asked where we were going, and Matron said, "a Cathedral city near the fighting line." It must be Bayeux. I wondered idly as we drove along if the famous tapestry was still there or if Goering had confiscated it as he had done (so we are told) with so many works of art in France.

I was not prepared for the sights that greeted us as we neared Bayeux. The parting of clouds of dust revealed huge tanks on the side of the road, black from burning, dozens of them with the dead crews hanging half in and half out of the turrets and escape hatches. There was mile after mile of destroyed armoured cars, trucks of all kinds, and always the dust, heat and stench of decaying maggot-ridden bodies.

20 JUNE 1944. The Pioneer Corps[7] are our Armed Guards, rifles at the ready, standing on the edge of our compound. They are delightfully unmilitary, rather untidy soldiers. Many are basically conscientious objectors. They are multi-nationals from all walks of life, some very well educated and with useful specialist skills. There is an officer with an unpronounceable name whom I call "Chezzy". He has told me a little of the background of some of these men. Many were refugees from Germany before the war. Chezzy speaks fluent English and German, also Polish and Russian. I think he is a Polish Jew, loves music and is a professional pianist in civil life. He is short and dark with a big nose and the most beautiful deep brown eyes. Chezzy has so much warmth and personality that

[7] The Pioneer Corps acted as guards to the hospital

it knocks me over. Why are ugly men often more attractive than the handsome ones.

There was some rapid gunfire this evening in the vicinity of the farmhouse. A Pioneer Corps corporal found the sniper. He cannot be more than fifteen years old. He was wounded in the leg and ironically became our first casualty! Fritz told Chezzy when he was interviewed that he had been ordered to stay behind to "fight for the Fatherland". The wound in his leg is superficial — a flesh wound. Fritz is very high and mighty, the product of Hitler Youth I suppose but he did not refuse the food we offered. He was ravenous.

The Pioneer Corps completed our new canvas latrines today. There is alarmingly little privacy. Driscoll and I are reducing our fluid intake in order to minimise the embarrassment of being escorted to the latrines by an armed guard. (Matron's orders because of the snipers). There are some terrible jokes about "pot" shots.

21 JUNE 1944. The sterilising equipment on the wards is almost nonexistent, positively archaic. I am sure Florence Nightingale was better off in the Crimea. We have to put syringes and needles, dressings, forceps etcetera in spirit. This is a terrible fire hazard particularly under canvas. We have primus stoves for boiling dressing bowls, heating drinks, etcetera. I have been practising on one today and find it unpredictable, unreliable and dangerous unless one is very careful. It needs the most patient pumping and cajoling to get it to work. I am terrified that it is going to explode.

Gradually they acquired more patients, from both sides. Curiously, they seemed to work together as a team.

24 JUNE 1944. Hans brings me a cup of tea as I sit at my desk to read the night report. My mind wanders for a while as I think of this ward and my charges. This multi-national microcosm of a Europe at war is interesting and sad. A badly wounded cockney says "thanks mate" to Hans as he gives him tea and fixes his pillows. Why are they all tolerant of each other inside this canvas tent, and killing each other outside. The Germans will eventually go back to a POW camp in England, our severely wounded will go to a hospital in England as soon as an air-lift is available. The others we shall patch up as best we can and send them back to "Monty" on the "Front" to fight again.

Spent the morning doing dressings, giving injections and fixing up plasma drips.

26 JUNE 1944. Good news this morning, some replacement uniform and underclothes arrived from England including ghastly khaki knickers. These pants are hilarious, huge and elasticated at the waist and legs, but we could have hardly expected army-supplies to have equipped us with glamorous cami-knickers. It will be blissful to feel clean. My battle-dress is dirty and blood-stained. Hot water is such a luxury. We are becoming anxious about hygiene in general, particularly as some of the girls have developed a mild dysentery. We are so short of Sisters that we can not afford to have anybody off sick.

29 JUNE 1944. Len has had his leg sawn off above the knee. The anaesthetic was difficult because of his fractured ribs and difficulty in breathing. Col. Cordwell was just going to sew up the flaps of the stump when the Luftwaffe came over again; so he was bandaged up quickly, and returned to me on the ward. I continued with the plasma, and gave him morphine for the pain. He also feels pain in the non-existent leg.

The ward was a shambles by now, and I had ordered all the patients to wear tin hats as shrapnel was coming through the roof.

5 JULY 1944. We had a convoy of young Canadian casualties brought in this morning. I was called for duty at 3 a.m. and was appalled at seeing their condition when I entered the ward.

There were stretchers all down the middle of the tent, there were charred bodies everywhere, some were quiet and dying, others screaming with pain, all with severe burns.

Everybody had to help; "up" patients, orderlies and sisters "off duty", Pioneer Corps soldiers, and all available medical officers.

Their bodies were black, their appearance horrific. We gave them morphia and more morphia and watched helplessly as they died. We moved the dead out of the ward and got on with trying to save the living. They were all so young and frightened.

The extra beds were put up, and we cut off the remnants of their uniform and gently laid them naked on their beds. Coverings were not possible because they could not tolerate anything touching their bodies.

We tried to replace the fluid loss with intravenous plasma and saline, and we were glad of the human heat, generated by the over crowded ward. They were so cold. We gave them penicillin in the hope of preventing infections, but we are very conscious of the fact that this is the worst type of condition to deal with in our inadequate surroundings and with so little equipment.

A young officer, Jock McGabe, one of the few able to speak, told me what happened. There was bitter fighting somewhere near Carpiquet aerodrome. The Canadians wear a darker shade of khaki uniform to ours similar to the Germans. Our troops attacked them with flame throwers, thinking that they were an enemy target. Such is the stupidity and futility of war.

CHAPTER
EIGHT

Seeing it Through

For many women in Britain, perhaps the majority, the war boiled down to the business of "seeing it through", of coping with the problems of rationing, absent husbands and war work and waiting for the benefits of the postwar world promised by the politicians and the press. Their war work was unlikely to attract any headlines, but its value was no less negligible for that. However, by 1944 war weariness had set in. D-Day, on 6 June 1944, provided a huge uplift, but there was still a long-hard slog before "the lights come on again".

A week after D-Day the population of south-east England came under fire from Hitler's V-weapons. The first flying bomb chugged across the Channel in the small hours of 13 June, falling to earth at Swanscombe, near Gravesend. The "doodlebugs", as they were quickly nicknamed, thrust Londoners back into the front line. The Home Secretary, Herbert Morrison, warned: "When the engine stops and the light at the end of the machine is seen to go out, it may mean that an explosion will follow, perhaps in five to fifteen seconds."

The V-1 was an unnerving weapon, and Vere Hodgson

wrote in her diary on 8 July: "The atmosphere of London is changed now. We are back in the feeling of the Big Blitz. There is apprehension in the air. The buses are far from full in the evening. There is no doubt that thousands have gone, and many more go to the Shelters and Tubes fairly early. That is — as soon as they are opened." As the V-1 bombardment continued, Londoners learned to live with the new threat, just as they had soldiered on through the Blitz. Vere Hodgson had her first close encounter with a "doodle-bug" early in July.

7 JULY 1944. Very cloudy and wet all day. Good day for Flying Bombs. We had a quiet evening, but round about mid-night, when we had just turned in and I was about to doze off, the Alert went, and very soon we had two big WONKS — fairly near.

Now today I have really seen one. As I got the meat at the butcher's the Alert went. Half-way down the road I heard a thrum-thrum. But as it seemed a long way off I did not pay much attention. However, a platinum blonde on the other side of the road lifted her head from reading a letter, and shouted to me — "Can you see it?" I said NO. So she shouted COME OVER HERE. I crossed the road, and, between the clouds, sure enough, right over our heads, was a horrible BLACK THING. It gave me quite a turn. The Platinum Blonde pursued her way unmoved, still reading her letter. . . . I regret to say I rather hastened my pace, though I think there was little likelihood, when seeing it directly above you, that it would fall on you. But for all the Platinum Blonde seemed to care, it might have been raining rose petals on us both.

By September 1944, the V-1 launching sites in northern

France were being over-run by the advancing Allies. However, there was no respite for Londoners as on 8 September the first V-2 rocket fell on Chiswick with a detonation which could be heard all over the capital. As Kate Phipps recalled, "The V-2s are absolutely horrifying. They just arrive with an appalling bang and jump one nearly out of one's skin. In the Blitz the noise was fairly continuous, and the V-1s you could hear coming, but these bastards just arrive unannounced."

But there *were* worse horrors. As the Allied armies advanced into Germany in the spring of 1945, they uncovered the most hideous excesses of the Nazi regime. The concentration camp at Buchenwald was liberated by US troops on 11 April; Bergen-Belsen, over-run by the British followed on the 15th. Terrible scenes greeted the liberators; Iris Ogilvie was in the area just a few days later.

The order came for us to proceed to Celle, about twenty miles north of Hanover. This move was very significant, it was to be near Belsen, the concentration camp. Our officers were aware that the medical arrangements for dealing with the victims were in the hands of the RAMC, but as soon as they possibly could, they visited Belsen to offer assistance. It had been considered that myself and another would accompany them on this first visit, but it was decided at the last moment that we should not go.

When they entered the camp, although it was four days since the liberation, what they saw was horrendous. The dead were still being buried and hundreds of emaciated victims were near death. Dirt and excreta everywhere, although every effort was being made to make some improvement in the situation. The stench was overpowering, they were shocked and stunned, and, although experienced in witnessing disturbing scenes, they admitted being physically sick.

When they returned to the unit, we could see that they had been deeply affected. They told us what they had seen and we found it unbelievable. "Sunshine" mentioned one particular thing that has always stuck in my mind. He said he was walking past what he thought was a pile of old clothing when he saw movement. There were indeed more victims still alive.

It was decided to fly a few of the victims, who were in a better physical condition and able to make the journey, to a hospital in Belgium. I was asked the following day to assist in their care, transferring them from their stretchers on to a Dakota. I remember, while I was waiting, the dreadful smell in the atmosphere. Some of the pilots told us afterwards that when planes flew at a certain height over Belsen the stench would sometimes penetrate into the planes.

The ambulances arrived and I was apprehensive as the first stretchers were unloaded and placed on the grass near the Dakota. I went up to the first victim and was stunned. As more were unloaded, I looked around, they all had the same look. Most of them appeared like old men, but, when I read the medical cards, pinned on their clothing, I discovered they were mostly young. The extraordinary thing was, looking back, I don't think I smiled at any of them. I find that unbelievable and very sad now. I don't know whether I was too shocked or couldn't bring myself to smile, and yet I had smiled a great deal at some of the troops who had become serious casualties.

I felt so very inadequate. Their eyes, I think, were

the most haunting, staring and almost lifeless, there was no emotion. I don't know whether they realised what was going on. I did give them the odd drink and saw to their comfort on the stretchers. When the last was loaded on to the plane, we stood there until it had taken off. Our contact with them was so brief, it was over in no time, but we were deeply affected. I felt so very humble.

In Britain, meanwhile, people prepared to celebrate Victory in Europe. In a letter to friends overseas, Kate Phipps painted a detailed picture of Staffordshire village festivities on VE-Day, 8 May 1945. Wartime rationing and restrictions lent an air of determined improvisation to the proceedings.

Well, we are having our celebrations in two parts. Having our cake and eating it . . . only we ain't got no cake as someone put it at the "planning committee". Alsager and Radway have — "damn their black marketing hearts", someone said from the platform, fortunately too low to be heard.

Today it was Churchill's speech on the radio at 3 pm, followed by a thanksgiving service from an airfield . . . certainly the most appropriate place for such. Rather a wet day but cleared up in the afternoon and I took myself for a walk to look at the local decorations.

It may amuse you all in Canada to try and visualise this village. I call it "our village", although I am only a visitor here, having just got my discharge from the factory[1] and, incidentally, National Service, I pre-

---

[1] She had been working as a nurse in a Royal Ordnance Factory.

sume. But today since we all belong to "England" it is ours and I am accepted as part of the picture and welcomed to the festivities.

First of all there is our bonfire, prepared some days back, an excellent effort considering all the things we are not supposed to burn! Mainly hedge clippings and salvage, but I noted also some rather worm-eaten chairs, and of course a good sprinkling of forms (Civil Defence and Home Guard). Alas, we are not to have the Home Guard and senior Civil Defence in our local procession tomorrow, they are performing at the more exciting District "Do's" at Stoke. But I don't feel like standing for hours, possibly in rain, watching others processing and listening to the Mayor's speech. Here everybody is to process, strangers and locals alike, anyone who did anything towards the war effort . . . and haven't we all!

Our village stretches uphill in a ribbon development, and the gardens are looking their best. People have gone in for "patriotic windows", the contents ranging from toy battleships and Spitfires to photos of the monarchs (including Queen Victoria) and the Big Three (Churchill, Roosevelt and Stalin).

Then there are the red white and blue flower arrangements and the odd gimmicky crockery set-ups. It could be a competition for the best-dressed or most original window (wherever did they get them?) . . . white towels with blue slippers and a red child's ball . . . a blue cloth, two utility cups and a scarlet bulb bowl of belated hyacinths. And of course hanging out of the windows the inevitable "white flag" in the shape of a sheet or a pillow slip with an irregular "V" pinned on to it in any colour which happened to be handy. Some have just hung out coloured bath towels, souvenirs no doubt of a happier couponless age. And a few have little flags (all nations) left over from coronations and political elections. I saw one window full of medals — an old lady displaying her dead husband's decorations from the Kaiser's War.

On returning to my friend's place I found tea in progress and actually a little sugared cake each, not to mention lavish scones and real butter. However, I could have done without the latter — it was Irish and distinctly "high". I much prefer marg! I dropped into the Parish church to say a small thanksgiving. It has been left open for such, I gather. Recently so many churches have to be kept locked up on account of pilfering and removal of altar ornaments. Too bad.

A Bevin Boy[2] who is staying at the same house and I crept out to see the bonfire while the family was listening to the King's speech. It made a magnificent show and Hitler's effigy on top was cheered as it disintegrated in the flames. Fine but very wet underfoot and all the kids enjoyed the lemonade and buns of a sort, the adults being warmed up by tea in the Women's Institute urn carried from a neighbouring house by two strong men. "Very cosy", remarked an old lady. I wouldn't have put it that way, but it was fun. Having recently read again T. S. Eliot's poem "East Coker", I suddenly realised what

[2] A young man conscripted to work in the coalmines. Named after Ernest Bevin, Minister of Labour and National Service.

a very primitive rite we were taking part in. Bonfires are part of England.

In Germany Nora O'Connor was helping to pick up the postwar pieces as part of an UNRRA team. The immediate need for emergency relief in Europe was undertaken by UNRRA (United Nations Relief and Rehabilitation Administration), established in November 1943 to help refugees of the nations fighting the Axis. It was to become one of the agencies of the fledgling United Nations Organisation.

Financed principally by the United States, UNRRA supplied raw materials and equipment for rebuilding European industry, agriculture and communications and was also responsible for the care and resettlement of millions of refugees. By the summer of 1945 every fifth person in the western zones of occupied Germany was a refugee, known as "displaced person" or DP. Nora O'Connor's team was bound for a cluster of camps north of Frankfurt.

UNRRA Teams had been learning about Displaced Persons since October 1944. On April 9th 1945, we had our first sight of them.

Long before the Camp was ready for their reception three thousand arrived in American ten-ton trucks. Sardine tins would have been spacious by comparison. They tumbled out in their hundreds, men, women, children; bags, bedding, bicycles and bugs. Russians, Poles, French, Dutch, Belgians, Czechs. In theory they should have been deloused before anything else; in practice the DDT ran out after the first few hundred.

While it lasted, "Operation Disinfectant" was worth watching. Two queues formed in a large drill-hall. The leaders were squirted with DDT powder by an expert, in order to demonstrate the technique and *"pour encourager les autres"*. This manoeuvre was carried out with more precision than delicacy, the "gun" being plunged under the victim's clothing, and powder vigorously discharged down the back, down the front, and, finally, up each arm and leg, male and female alike.

Next came REGISTRATION. A welfare officer from another Team and I stationed ourselves on a landing, half way up a stone staircase and tried to start registering French ex-prisoners of war. It was chaotic and was later vividly described in the *Daily Herald* whose reporters were standing by, while we were trying, quite unsuccessfully, to collect our wits and those of the DPs. Most of the prisoners had been shut away for five years. They were dazed and hardly able to understand questions or give answers. Their uniforms were in rags.

It was pathetic to see old and young preparing to spend the night on floors, surrounded by their few, but treasured, belongings. We had no bedding to give them and even straw was in short supply. The situation reminded us only too clearly of the hordes of people camping out nightly in London's Underground. Food, in the form of stew, was dished out to the weary, waiting crowd in any sort of container which the individual could scrounge. In spite of their troubles, the DPs remained cheerful amid all the confusion. The barracks, built to house 2,500 Germans was now required to house 10,000 Displaced Persons.

Next morning we were told to leave at once for

Giessen, to take over a camp where Russian and Polish inmates were at one another's throats.

As we entered Verdun Barracks the square was crowded with DPs who surrounded our truck, chattering like monkeys and pressing their faces against the windows. . . .

The quarters into which we thrust ourselves, designed to hold seven people, were already occupied by fifteen and we, counting the now restored Deputy and Doctor, made it twenty.

Clearing our flat, while the original squatters found what accommodation they could, took a week. Eventually we had to expand further as we were using our bedrooms as offices, by the light of hurricane lamps after dark. Fighting inch by inch for "Lebensraum" we finally achieved one complete floor as living and working premises. Our situation was in no way eased by being told that there were two other camps under our jurisdiction, bringing the population up to 11,000.

Some UNRRA Teams reported on the horrifying conditions in which they found DPs; evidence of starvation and persecution; some dead, diseased or dying. We had none of this. Our charges were remarkably healthy and active. Their activities consisted largely in beating up local Germans and stealing their belongings.

Poles, like the Irish, are hard drinkers and, like the Irish, they can make their equivalent of "poteen" (alcohol distilled from potatoes.) We had located several "stills" round the camp and rendered them extinct. Strong words were spoken to the wrong-doers by the Director as to what would be done by any more distillers caught in the act. We had a shrewd idea that there were other stills very much extant, but WHERE?

The answer came dramatically when the top floor of one block caught fire. Smoke and flames issued from the building; beds, bedding, clothing, chairs, tables, chests of drawers, suitcases, in fact anything movable, came through the air. At one moment by far the greatest danger was from that of missiles rather than from the fire itself.

After what seemed an age, the local Fire Brigade extinguished the conflagration. Unhappy owners of flotsam and jetsam could be seen prowling around disconsolately trying to identify their chattels from among the sodden stacks on the flooded barracks square.

We had no more trouble from poteen distillers.

Death stalked many of the DP camps. Pip Christiansen, a Danish nurse who had joined UNRRA in April 1945, recalls a harrowing incident at a camp near Lübeck.

One day a Polish woman came to me, screaming that there was a woman who had kept a dead baby in her bed for three days. When I asked why, I was told that the baby's mother refused to bury the child without its traditional burial clothes — little white dress and gloves and a cap decorated with leaves.

I told the woman I would come to the hut in the camp as soon as I could. Then I phoned the Officers Mess, where I had a flat, and asked them to bring me a "Busy Lizzie" pot plant I had there. Next I rang the Welfare officer and asked for the little dress and gloves to be sewn up. They made the dress and gloves from some nappies they had and the cap from a scrap of denim. Then I found the grieving mother and said, "I have got all the things for your little one, let us take her to the sick bay." We dressed the baby and laid it out in the sick bay, the little cap decorated with leaves from my pot plant. Then we buried the child. In the camp we had only three coffins, a small one for babies, a medium-sized one for older children and one for adults. After each burial we used them again.

A few days later the father and mother came to me and gave me a photograph of their dead child, taken by a German photographer. They told me, "This is to thank you for what you have done." It was so sad, but only one sadness among many.

The war left no one untouched. Iris Ogilvie was one of the tens of thousands of women widowed during the conflict. In May 1945 she visited her husband's grave.

While we were in Fassberg, "Sunshine" had very kindly arranged, with the Dutch authorities, that I should return to Holland by air and visit Flushing, where my husband had been buried. He and Billie accompanied me in a Dakota. After landing in Holland we then proceeded by road to the flooded area of Flushing, which had been a deliberate Dutch defence policy. We were taken in a little boat, as arranged, along the flooded roads and streets. What a strange experience, it was so incredibly still and quiet, just the sound of the boat making its way through the water. The roof tops of the houses and buildings were at eye level, so unreal, almost like a dream. We reached the cemetery on high-ground, an island in miles of flooding. We walked slowly amongst the crosses marking the graves of service men. Quite soon I was able to place some flowers on the grave we had come to find, and pay my respects to the other members of the crew buried there. . . .

The personal losses that she suffered during wartime did not prevent Iris Ogilvie from acknowledging the benefits it also brought.

Many of us who witnessed the tragedies of war in its many aspects are grateful to have experienced the meaning of true comradeship and friendship and perhaps learnt, at least a little, of the value of compassion, forgiveness and humility.

ACKNOWLEDGEMENTS

The authors would like to express their particular thanks to the following individuals who have so kindly assisted in their various ways towards the research and compilation of this book.

Special thanks must be given to the staff of the following departments of the Imperial War Museum: Philip Reed, Assistant Keeper, and Roderick Suddaby, Keeper, and all staff of the Department of Documents. Also, Ray Allen in the Department of Exhibits and Firearms, Jane Carmichael and all staff in the Department of Photographs, Terry Charman in Printed Books, Mark Seaman in Research and Information, Jenny Wood and all staff in the Art Department.

In addition our thanks to Anne Commander, formerly of the IWM, Mrs Margaret Davidson and Mrs Sheila Parkinson of the Women's Transport Services (FANY), Jean Cowley, Mrs G. Feldmann, Mrs Margaret Feldon, Mr and Mrs Donald Furniss, Major-General L.W.A. Gingell of the Officers Pension Society, Mrs Peter Hardinge-Francis, Mrs Elizabeth Harrison and Air Marshal Lewis Hodges of the RAF Escaping Society, Daphne Hill, Mary Hood, Helen Irens, Liane Jones, Janet Knox, Claire Malim, Samantha Marr, Lynda Marshall, Eileen Moore, Mrs Jean Procter, Chairman, British Women's Land Army Society, Pat Richards, Edwina Rofe, Mrs Anne Royle-Bantoft, Mrs Ben Tomsett, June Ventris. Grateful thanks to Dorothy Calvert for entries taken from *Bull, Battledress, Lanyard and Lipstick* (New Horizon, 1978); Scolar Press for extracts from *Raiders Overhead* by Barbara Nixon; Hilda M. Proctor (Diana Hester) for permission to use extracts from her memoir *Land Girl*; Mrs Stanley White (Francoise Labouverie (Rigby)) for granting permission for use of extracts from her book *In Defiance*.

The authors would also like to thank all the women who gave permission to use their wartime papers. We are greatly indebted to them and to those members of their families who also made material available to us.

BIBLIOGRAPHY

Beauman, Katharine Bentley, *Partners in Blue: The Story of the Women's Service with the Royal Air Force.* (Hutchinson, 1971)

Calder, Angus, *The People's War* (Cape, 1969)

Calvert, Dorothy, *Bull, Battledress, Lanyard and Lipstick* (New Horizon, 1978)

Cookridge, E. H., *Inside SOE* (Arthur Baker, 1966)

Cooper, Alan W., *Free to Fight Again: RAF Escapes and Evasions* (William Kimber, 1988)

Darling, Donald, *Secret Sunday* (William Kimber, 1975)

Estcott, Squadron Leader Beryl, *Women in Air Force Blue* (Patrick Stephens, 1989)

Foot, MRD, *SOE in France* (HMSO, 1966) *Six Faces of Courage* (Methuen, 1978) *SOE: The Special Operations Executive* (BBC, 1984)

Harrison, Tom, *Living Through the Blitz* (Collins, 1976)

Jones, Liane, *A Quiet Courage: Heroines of the French Resistance* (Bantam, 1990)

Jones, R. V., *Most Secret War* (Hamish Hamilton, 1978)

Joseph, Shirley, *If Only Their Mothers Knew* (Faber & Faber, 1946)

Longmate, Norman, *How We Lived Then* (Hutchinson, 1971)

Mason, Ursula Stuart, *The Wrens 1917-1977 A History of the Women's Royal Naval Service* (Educational Exploration, 1971)

McBryde, Brenda, *Quiet Heroines, Nurses of the Second World War* (Chatto & Windus, 1985)

Nixon, Barbara, *Raiders Overhead* (Scolar Press, 1980)

Sackville-West, Vita, *The Women's Land Army* (Michael Joseph, 1944)

Sheridan, Dorothy (ed), *Women in Wartime* (Heinemann, 1990)

Taylor, Eric, *Women Who Went to War* (Robert Hale, 1989)

Warner, Lavinia (with John Sandilands) *Women Beyond the Wire* (Michael Joseph, 1982)

INDEX

Afrika Korps, 192-3,196

Air Raid Precautions (ARP), 55

air raid warnings, 21, 22

El Alamein, 121, 122, 192

Anti-Aircraft Command, 92-5

Auxiliary Fire Service (AFS), 55

Auxiliary Territorial Service (ATS), 27-33, 72, 74-7, 82-4

barrage balloons, 20, 84-8

Batstone, Stephanie, 77-82, 88-92

Battle of the Atlantic, 73-4

Battle of Britain, 49-55

BBC, 128, 142

Beekman, Yolande, 124-5

Bergen-Belsen concentration camp, 218-20

Bernhard, Prince of the Netherlands, 147

Bevin boys, 222

Bigwood, Miss M. H., 113-15

Bismarck, 118-19

blackout, 11, 16, 18

Blanc, Henri, 139-40

Bletchley, Park, 117-19

Blitz, 55-71

Blyth, Harold, 119n

Blyth, Margaret, 119-20

Briggs, Phyllis, 166-70

British Expeditionary Force (BEF), 25, 32, 40, 46

British Intelligence, 116-31

Brown, Shelagh, 164-6

Buchenwald concentration camp, 218

Buckingham Palace, 17

Bullwinkel, Vivian, 168-70

Calvert, Dorothy, 82-4, 93-5

Carter, D. J. "Panda", 74-7, 79

Catroux, General, 189, 191

Catroux, Madame, 191

"Chain Home" radar system, 50-2

Chamberlain, Neville, 1, 3, 8-9, 18-19, 20, 23, 26

Changi prison, 170

Charlton, Moyra, 6-8, 27-32

Chicken, Dora, 63-7

children, evacuation, 16-17

Christiansen, Pip, 226

Churchill, Sir Winston, 26, 45, 49, 117, 186, 220

concentration camps, 134-7, 218-20

conscription, 72

Cormeau, Yvonne, 123-31

Cox, Gwladys, 19-22, 25, 48, 61-3

Crum, Michael, 120

D-Day, 129-32, 133-4, 216
Dachau concentration camp, 137-8
Daladier, Edouard, 3
Donald, Ailsa, 120-3
doodlebugs, 216-17
Dowding, Air Chief Marshal Sir Hugh, 49
Dunkirk, 32, 40-7

Edwardes Jones, Margaret, 118-19
Eliot, T. S., 222
Elizabeth, Queen, 19
Emergency Medical Services Hospital, Ashridge Manor, 45-9
Enigma, 119
evacuation, 2, 16-17

FANY, 116
Feldon, Margaret, 74
Fiat Libertas, 141-2
Folmer, Joke, 141, 143-6
Free French 189, 190
Fruchaud, Colonel, 191, 195

gas masks, 2, 7
Gaselee, Sir Stephen, 118
Gemmeke, Jos, 149-50
George VI, King, 19, 54
Gestapo, 132, 136, 142, 152-4, 157, 159
Giles, Mollie, 197-208
Goering, Hermann, 50, 211

Government Code and Cypher School (GC and CS), 116, 118

Hadfield, Lady, 34
Hadfield Spears Front Line Surgical Unit, 34-40, 189-94
Hall, Vivienne, 3-6, 8-9, 11-12
Hart, Flight Lieutenant Thomas, 63-7
Hauman, Colonel Pierre (Etienne), 149-54
Hearn, Corporal Avis, 54-5
Hester, Diana, 103-9
Hitler, Adolf, 1, 3, 9-10, 26, 49, 55, 118, 119, 222
Hodgson, Vere, 48, 216-17
Hoelen, Dr, 147-8

Inayat Khan, Noor, 124-5
intelligence, 116-31, 146-59

Jadoul, Marie Eugénie (Minouchat), 155-6
Japan, 160-88
Jonge, Maria de, 175-88
Jongh, Andrée (Dédée) de, 131

Kempei-tai, 175-84

Labouverie, Françoise, 149-54
Land Girls, 103-6, 107-8

Lawrence-Smith, Elizabeth, 92
League of Nations, 189
Lind, Nel, 141-6
Luftwaffe, 40, 50-4, 55, 59
Lynn, Vera, 140, 142

Maginot Line, 26
Maitland Wilson, General, 189
Mappin and Webb, 60
Maquis, 129-31, 132
Mata Hari, 166
Mellish Graham, Lord, 39
MI6, 155
Miles, Constance, 10-11, 17-18, 54-5
Milice, 128, 132
Ministry of Agriculture, 102
Montgomery, Field Marshal, 192
Moore, Eileen, 84-8
Morrison, Herbert, 216
Moubray, Mrs de, 163-4, 170
Mulrey, Mary, 69-70, 209-15
Munich crisis (1938), 1, 2-6, 8-9, 119
Muntok camp, 161, 166-7
Mussolini, Benito, 3

Nazareth British Military Hospital, 190
Nikis, Mario, 131-4
Nixon, Barbara, 56-61
Normandy landings, 197-215
nurses, 189-215

O'Connor, Nora, 223-6
Ogilvie, Iris, 197-208, 218-20, 227-8
Operation Dynamo, 40
Operation Overlord, 197-212
Operation Sealion, 49
OSS, 149

Page, Dennis, 120
Park, Air Vice-Marshal Keith, 50
Pearce, Josephine, 13-15, 34-40, 189-96
Pearl Harbor, 160
Phillips, Mrs, 41-5
Phipps, Kate, 15-16, 22-4, 26-7, 41-9, 59, 218, 220-3
"Phoney War", 25-6
Pioneer Corps, 214-15
police, 17
Prisoners of War, 110-11, 114
PTT (Postes, Télegraphies, Télécommunications), 131-2

radar, 51-4, 92-5
rationing, 25
Ravensbrück concentration camp, 134-7
Red Army, 196
Red Cross, 137, 159, 169
refugees, 29-30, 223-7
Reilly, Mrs M. M., 162
Resistance, 131-59
Rommel, Field Marshal, 192-3, 195

Roosevelt, Franklin D., 221
Royal Air Force (RAF), 25, 40, 73, 155
  Bomber Command, 55, 95-9
  Fighter Command, 49
Royal Navy, 39, 72-3

Sachsenhausen concentration camp, 136
shelters, air raid, 20, 54
Singapore General Hospital, 163-4
sirens, 23, 56
Spears, Mary, 34, 38
Special Operations Executive (SOE), 116-17, 123-30, 149
Stalin, Josef, 10, 221
Starr, George (Hilaire), 123, 126, 130
Stone, Frances, 99-101
Strachey, Oliver, 120

Tattersall, Emma, 131-8, 156
Tégal network, 149-55
Telecommunications Centre Middle East, 122-3
Territorial Army, 12
Terwindt, Trix, 142, 148n
Thomas, Sir Shenton, 162
Tjipinang, 184-5
Tompkins, Gladys, 170-4
Train Fantôme, 149, 155, 158-9
Tranberg, Yvette, 138-41
trenches, 12, 22

Trevor-Roper, Hugh, 120
Turner, Dame Margot, 168

UNRRA, 223-8
US Army, 111-13

V-weapons, 149, 216-17
VE-Day, 220-3
Veazey, Rev. Christopher, 59, 67-9
Veazey, Joan, 59, 67-9
Voluntary Front Line Surgical Unit, 34-40, 189-96
Vucht concentration camp, 143-4
Vyner Brooke, 164-6

Watson, Grace, 95-9
Watson-Watt, Robert, 131
Westminster Hospital, 15-16
White, Miss J., 109-13
Women's Auxiliary Air Force (WAAF), 49-54, 72, 75, 80, 84-8, 95-101, 104, 107, 116, 123
Women's Land Army (WLA), 96, 102-9
Women's Royal Naval Services (WRENS), 72, 77-82, 88-92, 117
Women's Voluntary Service (WVS), 40-5

Zero, network, 155, 157

LARGE PRINT

ISIS publish a wide range of books in large print, from fiction to biography. A full list of titles is available free of charge from the address below. Alternatively, contact your local library for details of their collection of ISIS books.

Details of ISIS unabridged audio books are also available.

Any suggestions for books you would like to see in large print or audio are always welcome.

ISIS
55 St Thomas' Street
Oxford OX1 1JG
(0865) 250333

General Non-Fiction

Richard Mabey	Home Country
Desmond Morris	The Animals Roadshow
Desmond Morris	Dogwatching
Frank Muir & Denis Norden	You Have My Word
Shiva Naipaul	An Unfinished Journey
Colin Parsons	Encounters With the Unknown
John Pilger	A Secret Country
R W F Poole	A Backwoodsman's Year
Valerie Porter	Faithful Companions
Sonia Roberts	The Right Way to Keep Pet Birds
Yvonne Roberts	Animal Heroes
Anne Scott-James	Gardening Letters to My Daughter
June Whitfield	Dogs' Tales
Ian Wilson	Undiscovered

Isis
Reminiscence
Series

The ISIS Reminiscence Series has been developed with the older reader in mind. Well-loved in their own right, these titles are chosen for their memory-evoking content.

Fred Archer	**Poachers Pie** *
Eileen Balderson	**Backstairs Life in a Country House**
Alice Thomas Ellis	**A Welsh Childhood**
Ida Gandy	**A Wiltshire Childhood** *
Bill Naughton	**On the Pig's Back, An Autobiographical Excursion** *
Diana Noel	**Five to Seven** *
Walter Rose	**The Village Carpenter** *
Jan Struther	**Try Anything Twice**
Flora Thompson	**Heatherley**
Alison Uttley	**Country Things** *
Alison Uttley	**Wild Honey**

* Available in Hardback and Softback

BIOGRAPHY AND AUTOBIOGRAPHY

Lord Abercromby	**Childhood Memories**
Margery Allingham	**The Oaken Heart**
Hilary Bailey	**Vera Brittain**
Trevor Barnes	**Terry Waite**
Winifred Beechey	**The Rich Mrs Robinson**
P Y Betts	**People Who Say Goodbye**
Sidney Biddle Barrows	**Mayflower Madam**
Christabel Bielenberg	**The Past Is Myself**
Ian Botham	**It Sort of Clicks**
Michael Burn	**Mary and Richard**
Winston S Churchill	**Memories and Adventures**
Denis Constanduros	**My Grandfather**
George Courtauld	**Odd Noises From the Barn**
Mary Craig	**The Crystal Spirit**
Dalai Lama	**Freedom in Exile**
W H Davies	**Young Emma**
Diana Farr	**Five at 10**
Joyce Fussey	**Calf Love**

BIOGRAPHY AND AUTOBIOGRAPHY

Joyce Fussey	Cats in the Coffee
Joyce Fussey	Cows in the Corn
Valerie Garner	Katharine: The Duchess of Kent
Jon & Rumer Godden	Two Under the Indian Sun
William Golding	The Hot Gates
Michael Green	The Boy Who Shot Down an Airship
Michael Green	Nobody Hurt in Small Earthquake
Unity Hall	Philip
Unity Hall & Ingrid Seward	Royalty Revealed
Thor Heyerdahl	The Kon-Tiki Man
Clive James	Falling Towards England
Clive James	May Week Was in June
Penny Junor	Charles
Imran Khan	All Round View
Julia Keay	The Spy Who Never Was
Margaret Lane	The Tale of Beatrix Potter
T E Lawrence	Revolt in the Desert
Bernard Levin	The Way We Live Now
Joanna Lumley	Stare Back and Smile

BIOGRAPHY AND AUTOBIOGRAPHY

Vincent V Loomis with Jeffrey L Ethell	**Amelia Earhart**
Vera Lynn	**Unsung Heroines**
Eugene McCarthy	**Up 'Til Now**
Jeanine McMullen	**A Small Country Living Goes On**
Jeanine McMullen	**Wind in the Ash Tree**
Gavin Maxwell	**Ring of Bright Water**
Ronnie Knox Mawer	**Tales From a Palm Court**
Peter Medawar	**Memoir of a Thinking Radish**
Jessica Mitford	**Hons and Rebels**
Eric Newby	**Something Wholesale**
Christopher Nolan	**Under the Eye of the Clock** (A)
Gerald Priestland	**The Unquiet Suitcase**
Wng Cdr Paul Richey	**Fighter Pilot**
Siegfried Sassoon	**Memoirs of an Infantry Officer**
Ingrid Seward	**Diana**
Frank and Joan Shaw	**We Remember the Home Guard**
Dolly Shepherd	**When the 'Chute Went Up**
Isaac Bashevis Singer	**Love and Exile**
Robert Westall	**The Children of the Blitz**
Ben Wicks	**The Day They Took The Children**

B/F